The Dynamics of Sango Language Spread

SIL International
Publications in Sociolinguistics

Publication 7

Publications in Sociolinguistics is a serial publication of SIL International. The series is a venue for works covering a broad range of topics in sociolinguistics. While most volumes are authored by members of SIL suitable works by others will also form part of the series.

Series Editor
M. Paul Lewis

Associate Editor
Gloria Kindell

Volume Editor
Marilyn Mayers

Production Staff
Bonnie Brown, Managing Editor
Karoline Fisher, Compositor
Hazel Shorey, Graphic Artist

The Dynamics of Sango Language Spread

Mark E. Karan

SIL International
Dallas, Texas

© 2001 by SIL International
Library of Congress Catalog No: 2001081408
ISBN: 1-55671-122-0
ISSN: 1091-9074

Printed in the United States of America

All Rights Reserved

06 05 04 03 02 01 00   10 9 8 7 6 5 4 3 2 1

No part of this publication may be reproduced, stored in a retrieval system, or transmitted in any form or by any means—electronic, mechanical, photocopy, recording, or otherwise—without the express permission of SIL International, with the exception of brief excerpts in journal articles or reviews.

Copies of this and other publications of SIL International may be obtained from

International Academic Bookstore
SIL International
7500 W. Camp Wisdom Road
Dallas, TX 75236-5699

Voice: 972-708-7404
Fax: 972-708-7363
Email: academic_books@sil.org
Internet: http://www.sil.org

Contents

List of Tables and Figures	ix
1 Introduction	1
2 Background	5
Political history of Sango	6
Literature concerning the use and spread of Sango	8
Samarin 1955	8
Jacquot 1961	12
Taber 1964 and 1979	14
Samarin 1986	15
Gerbault 1987	16
Moser 1992	16
Koyt 1994	18
Language spread	19
3 Quantitative Approach Orientation	27
4 Sentence Repetition Tests (SRTs)	33
5 The Development of the Sango SRT	47
Two-value scoring systems	48
Choosing the final fifteen sentences	50
Difficulty levels as a criterion of choice	54
SRT final form—RPE correlation	54
Conclusions concerning modifications of SRT procedures	56
Data gathering and coding	56

6 The Treatment of SRT Data: Social Factors 61
   Analysis of variance (ANOVA). 61
   Regression analysis 62
      Gender 64
      Age 65
      Occupation 67
      Residence 69
      Residence history. 69
      Parents' language. 70
      Spouse's language 71
      Education 72

7 The Treatment of SRT Data: The Effect of Language
   Differences on Bilingualism 75
   Genetic differences and bilingualism 76
   Geographic distance and bilingualism. 80

8 Participant Observation and Census Data 83
   Participant observation—gender 84
   Participant observation—schools 85
   Participant observation—attitudes toward languages 87
   Census data—distribution of Sango speakers 89

9 Observations and Conclusions 95
   The spread of Sango. 95
   The character of language shift: individual based. 95
   Distribution of social correlates. 96
   Language similarities and language shift. 97
   Motivations of language shift. 97
      Communication 97
      Economic gain 98
      Social Advantage. 98
      Religious motivations. 99
      Mimicry 99
   Language loyalty 100
   The SRT 100
   Summary. 101

10 Contributions to the Theory of Language Shift, Language
   Change, and Implications for Language Planners. 103
   Inevitability of the continuation of language spread. . . . 103
   Linguistic diversity, economics, and age of countries . . . 104
   Governmental and institutional considerations 106

Language planning through personal motivation
    modification 108
Ways to encourage the spread of a language 109
    Communication motivations. 109
    Financial motivations. 110
    Social motivations 111
    Religious motivations. 112
Ways to discourage the use of a language 112
Implications concerning language loyalty 113
Recommendations for literacy work. 115
Implications concerning language change 116
    Domain of language use or custom. 117
    Motivations of change 118
    Language as a social organism. 118
    Language acquisition process 119
    Labov's four problems 120
Conclusions 121

Appendix 1: Interlinear Texts 125

Appendix 2: RPE Proficiency Evaluations Wording. 133
    Descriptions pour l'évaluation des compétences dans le
        domaine de l'accent 133
    Descriptions pour l'évaluation des compétences dans le
        domaine de la grammaire 133
    Descriptions pour l'évaluation des compétences dans le
        domaine de facilité d'élocution 134
    Descriptions pour l'évaluation des compétences dans le
        domaine de vocabulaire 134
    Descriptions pour l'évaluation des compétences dans le
        domaine de compréhension. 135

Appendix 3: Second Language Proficiency Levels Descriptions .. 137

Appendix 4: Individual Subject SRT Scoring Sheet. 139
    Teste de Bilinguisme en Sango - SRT 139

References 141

Index 149

List of Tables

2.1	Sango use in Gbeya-speaking areas (Samarin 1955:265)	11
2.2	Sango use in different communication situations (Moser 1992:119–120)	17
2.3	Sango and French usage in communication situations (Koyt 1994)	19
4.1	Interpretation of coefficient of correlation	35
4.2	RPE point values for proficiency descriptions	41
4.3	Second language proficiency levels and RPE scores	41
4.4	Radloff's hypothetical example of discrimination index calculations (1991:57)	44
4.5	Examples of calculation for discrimination index and difficulty level (Radloff 1991:58)	45
5.1	Data fields included in coding	58
6.1	ANOVA for SRT	62
6.2	Regression analysis	63
6.3	Strength of effect of independent variables	64
6.4	Mean SRT by education and Bangui residence	74
7.1	Linguistic relatedness cluster analysis	79
10.1	Language heterogeneity and economic development (Coulmas 1992:24)	105

List of Figures

2.1	Ruben's decision-making tree (1968:526)	21
4.1	Linearity	36
4.2	Non-linearity	36
4.3	Homogeneous variance	36
4.4	Heterogeneous variance	36
4.5	Scattergram SRT long form and RPE	42
5.1	SRT-15 by RPE: Sentence chosen with predictability index and individual charts	53
5.2	Final SRT-15 RPE correlation	55
6.1	SRT by gender and age	65
6.2	SRT by age	66
6.3	SRT by occupation	68
6.4	SRT by residence	69
6.5	SRT by residence history	70
6.6	SRT by parents' language	71
6.7	SRT by spouse's language	72
6.8	SRT by education	73
7.1	Genetic tree of CAR languages	77

7.2 SRT by genetic relatedness of language 80
8.1 Percentage of Sango speakers per village 90
8.2 CAR map from The 1996 Grolier Multimedia
     Encyclopedia 91

1
Introduction

Language spread is the expansion of a language. It is the phenomenon of a language being used in a particular domain or geographic location where it had not been used in the past. Language spread normally occurs simultaneously on the geographical and domain-of-use axes. As a language spreads, it is used in ever-widening geographical locations. At the same time, it is used in ever-widening domains of language use within one geographical location.

Language spread does not occur unless there is a complementary language decline or retraction. Those geographical areas where a language is spreading, i.e., where it is starting to be used as an innovation, used a different language in the past. Those domain-of-use to which a language is spreading were, in the past, theaters of a different language. Thus, whenever a language is spreading, either geographically or within one community through expanding the domains-of-use, another language is retracting.[1]

Language spread, thus, is a concept that is used when one is focusing on one language. It is a useful term and concept in some realms, but one which I feel is not totally adequate when discussing the dynamics of a situation where new choices are being made in the realm of language use. Such choices are made between different alternatives, and in this case, the different alternatives are different languages. The shortcomings of the

---

[1] A situation where there is a genesis of a pidgin language would be an exception to the concept of there always being a language retracting for each expansion of a language. In a pidgin genesis situation, newly created social situations create the need for a new means of communication, thus the formation of the pidgin. In this case, there would not necessarily be a retraction of a language to correspond to the spread of the pidgin. The new pidgin would be used in previously nonexisting domains.

concept "language spread" stem from the one-language based perspective, as opposed to a wider perspective.

Examining language expansion and language retraction, as it happens at the same time (L1 spreading, L2 retracting), provides a better arena for understanding and discussing the rationale and motivations of what is actually happening. Thus, the concept of language shift, where one language replaces another in geographical and/or domain-of-use realms, is a better concept to use in discussing the dynamics of the spread of any one language.

Concepts such as relative prestige between two languages, or associations of particular languages in a community with values or dispositions or mind-sets, can only be profitably examined when investigating a change in language use from the societal viewpoint that does not only see one language expanding, but also sees the other language retracting.

This work is a study of language spread, from a language shift perspective. In order to do justice to the study of the motivations, social correlates, and determinants of language spread, a language shift perspective is necessary. This entails a study of the societal picture to best collect the data which would bring about meaningful insights.

The basic goal of this work is a fuller understanding of the dynamics of language spread. Hopefully, such an understanding will be of use in future endeavors in language development, engineering, and preservation.

This work is based on data collected during a four-year stay in the Central African Republic, and on data provided through census data from the Central African Republic (CAR) (Recensemaent générale de la population 1988). The data collected during the stay in CAR is of two types, a language proficiency test administered to over 700 people from whom social information was also collected, and participant observation.

Chapter 2 first gives background on the situation of the Sango language in CAR, and then enters into a discussion of the literature on language shift.

Chapter 3 investigates the similarity between language shift and language change—the language specific internal modification that is a normal phenomenon and which has been extensively studied. A parallel is drawn between the distribution of sociolinguistic variables in language change, and the distribution of sociolinguistic variables correlating with proficiency in the spreading language in language shift. The perspective of investigating language shift from an individual motivation perspective is also introduced.

Chapter 4 introduces memory tests and specifically Sentence Repetition Tests (SRT), the testing device developed and used to test proficiency in

Sango. As this SRT diverged from the normal pattern of developing an SRT (Radloff 1991), chapter 4 presents the canonical pattern of developing an SRT.

Chapter 5 discusses the actual development of the Sango SRT. The modifications to the design of the test and to the scoring system used are discussed. The design modifications seen as improvements to the original design were incorporated in the development of the Sango SRT. Chapter 5 also describes the actual application of the Sango SRT.

Chapter 6 discusses the results of the SRT data. The correlations of the different social factors are presented and discussed in light of the specific data patterns. Tentative explanations of the correlations are presented.

Chapter 7 investigates the effect that linguistic differences between languages might have on bilingualism. The SRT results are investigated in light of the genetic differences between the main household languages of the subjects and Sango in order to see if there is a correlation between genetic similarity of the household language and Sango.

Chapter 8 treats the data from the CAR census. Census data is used to graphically display patterns of bilingualism in Sango along with patterns of traditional language use. These data are compared to histories of transportation and Christian mission activity in the CAR. The census data are also compared to the SRT results, relying on insights supplied by the participant observation situations, in order to search for further insights into the dynamics of language spread.

Chapter 9 presents overall observations and conclusions to be drawn from the SRT data, from the census data, and from the participant observation. A framework of language shift is presented. It is hoped that this framework will provide an adequate foundation for discussion and intervention in language shift. By intervention in language shift I mean deliberate, planned activity with the goal of encouraging and advancing, or inhibiting and slowing language shift.

Chapter 10 discusses possible contributions to the theory of language shift. Emphasis is given to the implications of these contributions to the field of language planning and engineering. Practical suggestions for encouraging and inhibiting shift are given. Chapter 10 also investigates some parallels between what is being learned in the field of language shift and some theoretical problems in the area of language change.

It is hoped that this work will contribute in four areas. The first is the development of research tools enabling a quantitative study of language proficiency. The SRT is a good tool in such a study because it can accurately test language competency, since it has an application time of only ten minutes per test and thus allows a larger sampling of subjects to be tested for language competency.

The second area of contribution is that of providing insights into if and how genetic language differences affect bilingualism. How important are the linguistic differences between the traditional language and the new language in predicting bilingualism?

The third area of contribution is that of presenting a framework for better understanding, discussing, and working with the concepts of language spread and language shift.

The fourth area of contribution is that of providing insights into language development, engineering, and preservation. Along with this is an attempt to see if some of the insights might be applicable to language change.

2
Background

The Sango language is a lingua franca spoken in the Central African Republic (CAR). As of 1994, it is one of the two official languages of that country, the other being French.

Sango is based on a reduced form of an Ubangian language. Thus, it can be genetically classified as Eastern (or Ubangian) of Adamawa-Eastern of Niger-Congo.

Bruel (1935:165–6), as quoted in Samarin (1955:256), claims that Sango was already in use as a lingua franca before the arrival of French colonizing forces. The French occupation and colonization helped the spread of Sango because Sango speakers were recruited into the military from what was then the colony of Oubangui-Chari.

Sango was named after a language that was and still is spoken along the Oubangui River. This riverian Sango is distinct from the lingua franca Sango in that the riverian Sango is the traditional and active language of a small ethnic group. The lingua franca Sango was distinguished from the other Sango by the appellation, *sango tî turûgu* 'Sango of the soldiers'. Thus, initially, in many parts of the CAR, Sango was associated with the speech of soldiers.

Today, most people refer to the Sango which is the mother tongue of that small group living near the Oubangui River as riverian Sango, as opposed to simply Sango, the lingua franca which is becoming the mother tongue of an ever growing portion of the population in the CAR.

In my stay in the CAR, I have often heard the following phrasing, in French or in Sango, also used to refer to the lingua franca Sango in an unambiguous way: Sango of the market, Sango of Bangui, vernacular Sango, popular Sango, national Sango, street Sango, commercial Sango, official Sango.

Samarin (1982) also maintains that Sango must have already been in use when the first colonists arrived. He bases this idea on the absence of influences from Gbanziri on the lingua franca Sango. Gbanziri was the language of the group that transported the first Europeans to the area. Samarin maintains that if there was no lingua franca already in use, a language developing at the time of contact with the first Europeans would have more Gbanziri influences.

Pierre Kalck states that a "riverine canoeing people", the Sango, traded on many northern branches of the Ubangui River system before the French occupation, and that the Sango language was known in "these different valleys" (1980:119). He also states that, connected to the French occupation, the Sango language "became the lingua franca for all of the Ubangui-Shari territory" (1980:119).

In his 1955 article, Samarin states that the lingua franca apparently is derived from the language of the same name, which in turn is one of the dialects of a language group consisting also of Ngbandi and Yakoma (1955:256). However, later in the same work, in discussing the structure of Sango as compared to the structure of its mother language, he treats Ngbandi as the mother language of Sango (1955:260).

Bouquiaux and Diki-Kidiri (1978:8) sidestep the issue of the mother language of Sango by stating that Sango is "a language of the Ubangian group related to Ngbandi".

The most popular viewpoint today of the origins of Sango are that the language developed as a lingua franca from a pidginized form of one of the languages in the Ngbandi-Yakoma-Sango language group (Niger-Congo, Adamawa-Eastern, Eastern, Ngbandi-Yakoma-Sango), and that this African-based pidgin went through a creolization process (Holm 1989:562–563).

Political history of Sango

In November 26, 1964, a constitutional law was passed (number 64/37) making French the "official language" of the country, and Sango the "national language". This occurred after David Dacko was elected president (January 5, 1964) and the new constitution, proposed by Dacko, was adopted (November 20, 1964). A few months later, on January 15, 1965 a commission to study Sango (Commission Nationale pour l'Etude de la Langue Sango) was established under the Minister of Education (Ministère de l'Education Nationale).

In 1974, a national pedagogical institute was created. This institute was given the task of preparing the introduction of Sango into the formal and non-formal education systems. It was founded at a time when relationships between CAR (then the Republic of Central Africa) and France were at a low point. On May 16, 1974, the Central African government forced the closing of the French consulate general, and on May 27, 1974, President Bokassa accused France of having initiated a plot against his life.

The institute carried out a pilot program in 1975 of around 150 classes, which introduced Sango in the first few years of education in the school system. The program failed, and for years acted as a deterrent to primary and/or bilingual education in Sango.

Koyt attributes the failure of the pilot program to a lack of a *préparation sérieuse et de programmation rigoureuse* (1994:8). He also states, *nombreux été les parents d'élèves qui ont marqué leur réticence à légard du project, ayant été peu or pas suffisamment sensibilisés à la question* (1994:8). Many parents were reluctant to allow their children to enter or continue in such classes because they felt that by being in such a bilingual classroom their children would be disfavored and disadvantaged in learning French, and thus be disadvantaged and disfavored in life. This attitude of the parents is erroneous in that research in bilingual education has shown that children who start their education in a language they understand well, and transition to a language of wider communication which they know less well, control the language of wider communication better at the end of three years than students who had been educated exclusively in that language.

In 1975, the Institute de linguistique appliquée (ILA) was created as a research branch of the University of Bangui. Koyt describes the charter of the ILA as:

1. Contribuer à assurer l'étude des langues et traditions orales centrafricaines;
2. Suivre l'évolution de la situation linguistique nationale;
3. Assurer l'exécution de la politique linguistique nationale. (1994:17)

The ILA is involved in many different research and development projects, many of which are studying Sango. There is a lot of work going on in the area of creation of new terms in Sango and in the description of Sango.

In 1981 Des Etats généraux de l'éducation, a type of national board of education, met to discuss the place of Sango in education in the CAR. Their findings were published in Ordinance no. 84.036 of May 15, 1984. Article 36 of this ordinance states, *l'enseignement est dispensé en français langue officielle et en sango, langue nationale* (Koyt 1994:8) (both French [the offical language] and Sango [the national language] will be used in the educational institutions). Koyt notes that this is the *de jure* situation, but the de facto state is that education is carried out only in French. He does state that teachers sometimes fall back on Sango when the students are unable to understand an idea in French, but that this practice is severely frowned upon by the education inspectors. My own experience has led me to believe that this practice of falling back on Sango is much more common than the education inspectors would like to admit. As Sango is seen as a unifying national language, there is a certain pride and prestige in propagating Sango. If such propagation is present, it is *sub rosa* because of the French government's influence on, and funding of, national education in the CAR.

In January of 1984, decree no. 85.025 established the official orthography of Sango.

In 1991 constitutional changes were enacted where Sango was given the status of an "official language". At the same time, the other languages spoken in the country were recognized as "national languages". This results in a situation where there are two "official languages", Sango and French, and one of the two, Sango, is also a "national language". The languages of the different ethnic groups are also "national languages".

Literature concerning the use and spread of Sango

Samarin 1955

Samarin, in 1955, wrote a good description of different sociolinguistic aspects of the Sango language. Concerning the origins of Sango, he wrote:

> The Sango dialect "widely distributed" (Greenberg, Language) on both sides of the Ubangi river approximately at the confluence of the Mbomu and Uele rivers, was first learned by neighboring groups, such as the Buraka (and even by the Gbanziri). For, as Bruel explains (1935:165-6), these people were already using Sango at the time of the arrival of the French colonizing forces. It was then spread *"un peu partout"* following the French occupation, because the French recruited their first military forces *("miliciens"),* canoers, and assistants to the merchants from among the people living along the Ubangi river....Since then Sango has been utilized as a medium of communication by Africans and to some extent by Europeans wherever European business, whether political or economical,

has congregated Africans speaking different languages. (1955:256–257)

Concerning the similarity between Sango and Ngbandi, Samarin (1955:260) describes a short study that he conducted comparing the two languages. He states, "Ten hours of work with an informant revealed remarkable similarity in vocabulary, syntax and phonology." He reports that a major difference between the two languages is the simplification that occurred in Sango where it lost morphemic use of tone, whereas in Ngbandi, grammatical tone markings on verbs and pronouns indicate verbal aspects (Nelson 1952).

Samarin (1955:260) goes on to note that, despite the similarities between Ngbandi and Sango, the two languages are not mutually intelligible. The speakers of the Ngbandi understand the lingua franca Sango, but speakers of Sango do not understand Ngbandi.

Concerning the influence of the French language on Sango, Samarin (1955:261) states that Sango is unusually and relatively free from French influences, what influences there are being only lexical. He states that Sango has not acquired any French phonemes and those who do not speak French do not use many French-based words. There is more use of French-based words where there are colonistic influences and presence than in the "bush".

He does note that there is a section of the population who introduces more French into Sango than other sections of the population. He states, "the Sango of those who have had more than a smattering of French but no formal education is almost unintelligible for the haphazard use of French expression" (1955:261). This is probably due to the high status of French at that time. Those people who knew some French, but who hadn't had the opportunity to learn French fully, would desire to demonstrate their knowledge of French in an attempt to improve their status and social standing by using as much French as they could. I believe what Samarin is describing could well be a code-switching situation where there was incomplete acquisition of one of the codes involved, French.

Concerning the spread of Sango, Samarin (1955:260) states that the spread of Sango to the Buraka and Gbanziri speaking regions, as well as to the Ngbandi region, was facilitated by the congruent structures and close genetic relationship of all these languages.

> Since the occupation of Oubangui-Chari there has been no arresting the spread of Sango. Once it had arisen and had been sufficiently modified so as to be easily and quickly learned, it has spread in step with every European development of the territory. Every African who desires to share in what the new

way of life has to offer, which is found mostly outside the "bush" villages, must almost necessarily learn Sango in order to communicate with those Africans who represent the government or the various commercial firms. In addition, the Christian missions, both Catholic and Protestant, in the absence of a people literate in French, as Kérot has so clearly explained, must necessarily resort to Sango. (1955:258)

Samarin reports that in 1955 Sango was being used as a language for inter-group contact. He states that it is used not only for contact between people with different mother tongues, but that it is also used between people that speak different, but intelligible, dialects of the same language (1955:264).

Concerning the prestige of Sango, Samarin writes:

Sango seems to share with French in being an "upper" language of the area. There seems to be a conscious effort on the part of most people to learn Sango. It is a language of prestige, not because the European uses it, but because it is used by the culturally superior inhabitants of the posts. This superiority is mainly a question of having clothing. The person who is ignorant of Sango is classed as somebody from the "bush", which is equivalent to saying that he is a "hick". The ideal is, of course, French. In practice, however, Sango is more important. It enables one to acquire a wealth that he would not quickly or ever acquire if he had to depend on a knowledge of French which, to most people, is not easily obtained. (1955:262–263)

Thus, Samarin reports that Sango is a prestige language of the area, along with French, but more accessible than French, which would require years of formal schooling to master. The African social elite spoke French and Sango, but reserved the French for communication between their clique. He reports that there are negative social connotations of not knowing Sango and that there are positive financial ramifications of knowing Sango.

Samarin spent most of his time in Africa in Gbeya-speaking areas. In discussing whether or not Sango is a dominant language in relation to the mother tongue Gbeya (Gbea), Samarin presents the chart in table 2.1, based on the criteria for a dominant language presented by Weinreich (1953:75–9).

Table 2.1 Sango use in Gbeya-speaking areas (Samarin 1955:265)

	Bush Sango	Bush Gbea	Bangui Sango	Bangui Gbea
Relative proficiency	+	+	+	+
Mode of use (visual)	+		+	
Order of learning		+	+	+
Usefulness in communication		+	+	
Emotional involvement		+		+
Function in social advance	+		+	

From this chart, it is evident that Sango demonstrates a certain dominance in Bangui, not even considering its function in economic advance nor its function in religion. In the bush areas, it would also be possible to envisage a growing dominance of Sango, especially in light of its place in social, economic, and religious advancement.

Samarin states that already in 1955 there was a growing loyalty to Sango due to religious factors. He states that, "Some Africans feel that the native languages tend to divide the people whereas Sango unites them all into one Christian body" (1955:264). He goes on to say that, "there is some evidence to indicate that Sango has come to be identified, at least among the Protestants, as the Christian language, so that many people are inclined to pray, preach, or study the New Testament in Sango" (1955:264).

Samarin presents an illustration of this where Sango was considered the Christian language associated with God, and the local language was considered a pagan language associated with the Devil. He states that a man who spoke Kare as his mother tongue recounted a dream to him where God spoke to him in Sango and the Devil spoke to him in Kare (1955:264).

Another important association that Samarin presents is the association of Sango with modern Africa, while the mother tongues are associated with rural, backwards Africa (1955:264). As prestige in Africa often goes along with the idea of being current, modern, and urban, this association of Sango with the modern is seen as an important factor in a motivating shift toward Sango. In discussing the usage of Sango in 1955, Samarin states:

> Sango is by no means universally known, however. It probably can be said in safety, without the verification of any kind of definite survey, that in the "bush" children up to, say, ten years old and adults over, say, forty years do not speak Sango.

This observation, of course, will vary in validity from place to place. (1955:263)

He goes on to say, "More accurate is the observation that men and boys of any given age-group are better acquainted with Sango than are the women" (1955:263). He attributes this to the girls and women being less exposed to Sango than the boys and men. He describes the social situation where the men and boys are free to go to government schools, roam in town, and go on trips to visit people, while the women and girls are pretty much bound to the house.

He also discusses the possibility of women refusing to use Sango as it is a mark of advancement, and some women might want to be associated with cultural conservatism (1955:263). In today's Africa, identification with the modern and urban by women often includes the unwanted attributes of being considered less moral in sexual realms. Thus, it is not unreasonable that in 1955 some women would refuse to speak or learn Sango, or hide the Sango that they knew, because of an association with modern, urban life, which itself was associated with women with low morals.

In discussing the vitality of Sango, and the possibilities of its spread in the future, Samarin states, "The future of Sango is not at all bright. The French policy of not officially recognizing any language but French...permanently casts Sango as an inferior language" (1955:266–267). Samarin's mistake here was putting too much weight on French policy and opinion, an understandable mistake in the time before the modern independence movement in Africa. His prediction was poor, not because of a lack of understanding of the situation in the CAR, but because he could not imagine the changes of attitude that would be brought about with independence—changes that would strengthen the motivations that brought about Sango use and spread. Sango was already considered a language of modern Africa. With independence, Sango began to be considered the language of national unity.

Jacquot 1961

In 1958, André Jacquot headed up a sociolinguistic survey in several of what he calls villages located in the northern part of the Bangui urban district. Bangui is the capitol of the CAR, and had a population of around 75,000 in 1958. The study, of which he published the results in 1961, was aimed at investigating the spread of Sango in the urban milieu, how and when it was learned, and whether it was used just in verbal form or if it was also read and written.

Jacquot's research design included employing two Central Africans to tag along with the national census that was in progress, and to ask questions of the subjects. He was able to get 1,412 interviews, with all the subjects from urban neighborhoods (villages) on the north end of the Bangui urban area. The subjects were first asked twenty-four questions concerning social factors such as sex, age, ethnic origin, place of birth, profession, etc., and then were asked a number of questions to determine their usage of Sango.

- *Quelle est la langue maternelle?*
- *Le sango est-il parlé, et dans l'affirmative où et comment a-t-il été appris?*
- *Dans quelles circonstances est-il habituellement utilisé (dans la famille, dans les relations avec les voisins, etc...)?*
- *Est-il seulement parlé, ou est-il également lu, écrit?*
- *Où cette connaissance a-t-elle été acquise?*
- *Quelles sont les autres langues connues?* (1961:160)

Of the 1,412 people surveyed, only one said that she did not speak Sango. This was a 22-year-old Manja woman who had recently moved from the Manja home area into a neighborhood that was ethnically Manja. Most of the subjects (1,295) declared that they learned Sango when they were children, and most of them also declared they learned Sango in their ethnic home area. Of the 1,412 subjects, only 116 (37 men and 79 women) declared that they learned Sango after they came to Bangui.

As Jacqot's sample contained 739 men and 673 women, this predominance of women who came to Bangui not knowing Sango indicates that there was a definite gender distinction in the distribution of rural Sango speakers at that time, confirming Samarin's deductions. Rural men did speak Sango more than rural women.

Jacquot makes two observations which are different than one would expect and would prove to be very important if verified by other research. One is that the factor of ethnicity affects bilingualism in Sango which is not at all uncommon since ethnic groups often show differing behaviors. The other is that Sango does not have any domains of use distinctions. However, the concept of DOMAINS OF USE distinctions in language choice in bilingual situations is seen worldwide.

Jacquot notes, *A l'époque actuelle le sango commercial semble d'un usage largement répandu dans l'ensemble du pays.* He also notes that Bangui, the cosmopolitan capital and center of attraction, provides the best conditions for the use of Sango (1961:158). Concerning the use of Sango as a mother tongue, he notes:

> *Le plus souvent, le sango est une seconde languge qui s'ajoute à la langue maternelle première langue. Cepandant cette situation paraît être en train de se modifier chez les enfants actuels qui connaissent fréquemment la langue véhiculaire mieux que celle du groupe auquel ils appartiennent par leur naissance. Ceci semble dû à la fréquentation de plus en plus nombreuse des établissements scolaires: les enfants de toutes origines qui se retrouvent dans les écoles n'ont souvent pour se comprendre que deux possibilités, qui sont l'usage du français it celui du sango. La facilité et la maniabilité du sango lui donnent la faveur pour les relations courantes et l'habitude se maintient pour l'enfant revenu dans sa famille.* (1961:163)

It seems that Jacquot oversimplifies the motivations of the choice between Sango and French when he says that Sango is chosen because it is easy to use and learn. Social pressures and motivations would also influence this choice. The maintenance of Sango at home, being carried over from the school, is also simplified by Jacquot as he attributes this to the habit of using Sango at school. Again, he is ignoring the social pressures and motivations that would influence the choice of Sango. However, the desire to communicate at school and with other ethnic groups would, as he states, have a very large part in motivating the switch to Sango.

Taber 1964 and 1979

Taber's 1964 and 1979 work was based on the corpus collected by Samarin in 1962. Taber's contribution was a statistical analysis of the French-based loan words found in the 1962 corpus, and then a dialogue on the motivations of the lexical borrowing that was very prevalent. Taber (1979:190) first presents Weinreich's (1953) seven reasons why lexical items are borrowed. Then, through the analysis of the loan words in the corpus, he gives strong support to one of Weinreich's reasons, and suggests that at least one more reason for borrowing must be allowed.

The reason of Weinreich's that Taber gives evidence for is the one of nouns coming into a language along with the introduction of the item referred to which is new to the culture. Weinreich gives the example of the "tomahawk" being introduced into English. Taber shows that texts that deal with Western topics have more French loan words than texts that deal with indigenous topics.

The new reason that Taber proposes is one of a grasping after "security", exercised by members of the society who have not obtained a position of power or prestige and who would desire such advancement. He contrasts a number of people in secure positions—a former president, a priest, a leader of a community agricultural project, and ten prestigious radio announcers—with people in less secure positions such as farmers, young storekeepers, and adolescent girls. He found that the insecure people used a great deal more borrowing from French than did the secure ones. Concerning the insecure, he states:

> In a situation where advancement and prestige are so completely tied to knowledge of French as in the Central African Empire, it is inevitable that they would be strongly motivated to display whatever French they knew. Note that this need not at all be a conscious decision. but is obviously a strong inner drive. (1979:197)

Taber associates this higher level of borrowing by the insecure with Labov's (1966) cross-over patterns of hyper-correction where members of the upper-middle class use less post-vocalic rs in casual speech than the upper class, but surpass the upper class in the use of post-vocalic rs in careful speech.

Taber concludes by stating:

> It seems clear from the present study that in addition to the motivations adduced by Weinreich to explain lexical borrowing, the drive of the insecure to gain security must also be considered an important factor, especially in any context where there is a great disparity of prestige between the two languages in contact. (1979:197)

Samarin 1986

Samarin's 1986 work concludes that the French that is being learned in the CAR is very close to the Parisian standard, but that there is no standardized or correct form for the Sango that is in use. He speaks of differences in Sango along the rural-urban axes, the protestant-catholic distinction, and the age dimension. He also wrote that in 1986 the urban variety of Sango had a "considerable admixture of French" which the rural people desired to emulate (1986:384).

My own observations in 1990–1994 were very different. I perceived that the urban population spoke Sango with fewer French loan words than did the rural population. It seems that there had been a major change. The urban populations adopted the viewpoint that it was not good to mix French with their Sango. The rural populations, however, had not yet had the opportunity to adopt this trend, and their speech was thus characterized as backward and rural by the city dwellers because of the high proportion of these previously prestigious French loan words.

At one point, in 1993, I observed three university students having a conversation in Sango and were competing to see who would be the first to use a French-based word. One of the men lost the game, after thirty-seven minutes! This illustrates the current desire to rid Sango of French-based words.

In traveling to rural areas, I often observed people from these areas complimenting the Sango of certain expatriates who learned their Sango in Bangui, the capitol. Typical comments were, "Oh, that Sango is so much better than mine, it is so pure" and, "That is very, very good Sango." The positive value attributed to French-free Sango seems to be spreading to the rural regions.

Gerbault 1987

Gerbault did a study of the use of Sango in Bangui and also noted some attitudes that were related with its use. She collected people's stated responses concerning their use of Sango and their attitudes toward its use. Her general conclusion is that in Bangui Sango is rapidly gaining ground that previously was held by vernacular languages. She found a positive attitude toward Sango, as demonstrated by a high percentage (83%) of those she surveyed desiring to see Sango used in elementary education.

Samarin (1986) uses some of Gerbault's findings to support his view that Sango did not have a generally accepted standardized form. He states that the relatively low responses given to Gerbault's question of how well the subjects spoke Sango, in a city where Sango was the major language of communication, indicate that there was some insecurity as to what "good" Sango was.

Moser 1992

In Moser's study concerning language use in different domains of use in the CAR (1992). She used a questionnaire which listed different communication situations. These she labeled domains of use. The situations which define her domains are mostly based on whom one is addressing. For instance, her domain "elderly" is defined by what language one is using when addressing older people. She traveled to many of the major cities of CAR to ask subjects to self report their language use for her different audience-defined domains of use.

Moser presents the data in table 2.2, showing the percentage of use of Sango in different audience-defined communication situations.

Table 2.2 Sango use in different communication situations
(Moser 1992:119–120)

		never	sometimes	often	always	missing
1.	Elderly	72.0	21.1	4.9	2.1	—
2.	Parent	78.6	16.3	3.8	1.3	—
3.	Sibling	61.7	24.5	9.8	4.0	—
4.	Children	40.5	33.9	17.1	8.4	—
5.	Spouse	58.3	23.3	10.2	8.3	—
6.	Friend	27.4	28.9	31.6	12.1	—
7.	Neighbour	47.0	25.2	14.0	13.8	—
8.	Work	48.7	24.2	17.1	9.7	0.2
9.	Chief	40.5	21.2	15.2	23.1	—
10.	Prayer	22.9	14.7	29.1	33.0	0.2
11.	Church	13.2	11.0	31.8	42.8	1.1
12.	Pastor	13.1	6.7	26.3	52.8	1.0
13.	Funeral	36.2	23.5	14.6	25.7	—
14.	Wedding	33.2	25.2	18.0	23.4	0.2
15.	Festival	40.8	30.0	17.6	11.5	0.1
16.	Hospital	7.0	5.8	29.1	58.1	—
17.	Doctor	7.8	7.3	24.8	60.0	—
18.	Nurse	6.7	6.1	22.0	65.1	—
19.	Admin	9.1	9.5	28.9	52.3	0.2
20.	Police	5.9	6.1	24.4	63.2	0.5
21.	Market	8.3	16.2	47.5	28.0	—
22.	Shop	5.6	6.6	25.2	62.5	—
23.	Post	*6.5	6.0	20.8	56.8	9.9
24.	Bank	*9.8	7.6	9.5	41.2	21.9
25.	Counting	40.4	30.4	20.2	9.1	—
26.	Dreaming	63.4	19.8	8.1	8.4	0.1
27.	Quarrel	49.1	28.3	12.1	10.5	—
28.	Healer	46.4	25.8	11.9	14.3	1.6
29.	Animal	65.4	17.3	62.2	10.6	0.5
30.	Water	46.6	29.0	15.8	8.6	—

* These are not valid percentages considering the large amount of missing values.

Moser states that Sango is spoken mainly in the following twelve environments: shop, police, hospital, nurses, post, doctor, administration, pastor, bank, market, church, prayer (1992:120). These are the environments in which inter-culture group contact is the most prevalent.

These findings contradict the earlier statement of Jacquot who surmised that Sango does not have any environments of use distinctions. Moser's work, however, as well as a short study by Wenezoui (1989), reveals that domains of use do have a considerable effect on the use of Sango. This is to be expected in light of normal patterns of domain-defined language use.

Koyt 1994

According to Koyt, the constitutional law that designated Sango to be an official language, alongside of French, was overdue and needed to have the *de jure* situation match the de facto.

> *La loi constitutionnelle no 64/37 du 26 Novembre 1964 confère au français le statut de langue officielle et au sango celui de langue nationale. Ce n'est que 27 ans plus tard, en 1991, que le sango sera promu au statut juridique de langue officielle de la république centrafricaine conjointement avec le français.*
>
> *Cette loi constitutionnelle conférent au sango le statut de langue officielle institue de jure un bilinguisme d'Etat, alors que le peuple, est plurilingue. Par ailleurs la majorité de la population s'exprime en sango et seule une minorité comprend et utilise le français.* (Koyt 1994:1)

His writing exhibits some of the sentiments concerning French and Sango which are prevalent in the CAR. Sango is seen to have been somewhat deprived of the recognition it deserves. French is seen to have been overemphasized. Sango is associated with the nation, French with France. Francophonization, deliberate attempts to increase the use of the French language and to consolidate a block of countries using that language, is often perceived as post-colonial oppression in countries such as CAR. This is especially true because typical methods of encouraging a language in past times included discouraging other competing languages.

Koyt states that Sango has become a factor of national cohesion and a symbol of Central African identity. He goes on to say that even though it has numerous social and regional varieties, Sango is fairly homogenous in that all the varieties are very similar.

Koyt also reports that there is a large amount of code-switching (Sango/French) and mixed language phenomena which is still in widespread use even though it is resisted by certain purists.

Koyt also describes the language-use situation in Bangui by detailing certain communication situations and activities, and then telling what languages are used in those situations or activities. I have prepared table 2.3 to display his findings concerning language use, extending the use of the word domain to include traditional domains, communication situations, and activities.

Table 2.3 Sango and French usage in communication situations (Koyt 1994)

Domain	Language
home	ethnic language and Sango (in Bangui)
neighborhood	Sango
children's games	Sango
school yard	Sango
school class	French and some Sango
government for administrators	French
radio	70% Sango, 30% French
television	French and Sango
newspaper	French
presidential speeches	French and Sango
judicial system	French with Sango translation if needed
national assembly	French and Sango
political parties	French and Sango
singing	Sango
theater	French and Sango
religion	Sango
religious literature	Sango
religious radio	Sango

Language spread

When languages spread, there is a shift in community language-use patterns. A useful tool in the discussion of language spread and language loss has been the concept of domains of use, introduced by Fishman (1964, 1965). Typical domains of use would be home and work. Domains would be seen as the conglomerate of factors which define typical communication situations: factors such as participants, location, topics of conversation, and formality level. In this approach, language spread is defined as when a particular domain calls for the use of the spreading language, whereas in the past a different language had habitually been used in that domain.

This domains approach is useful in demonstrating language shift over time. For instance, if language 1 was used in domain A ten years ago, and today language 2 is used in domain A, this would indicate the spread of language 2. However, this domains approach which summarizes the results of language shift from the community perspective, is of limited use in discovering or discussing the dynamics of language spread. I believe that an approach which is less based on the community, and more based on the individual, is needed for profitable discussion of the dynamics of language spread.

Rubin (1968) presents a "decision tree" which she states represents the language-choice decision-making process that certain Paraguayans employ (see figure 2.1). It appears to me that Rubin's tree describes the results of the decision-making process, and that the decisions themselves are more motivated by the communicative and social good of the speakers. For instance, according to Rubin's tree, the first thing that influences a speaker when deciding which language to use, Guarani or Spanish, is whether he or she is in a rural or non-rural location. This node in Rubin's tree is the top node because Rubin found that the most important factor in predicting what language would be used was that of whether the conversation was in a rural or urban area.

My surmise is that the speaker is not thinking about whether he or she is in a town or village, but rather is considering what should be done in order to have the desired communication and establish the proper social contacts. I propose that the speakers' quest for communicative and social good will cause him or her to use Guarani in rural locations and possibly Spanish in the non-rural situation, thus giving a basis for Rubin's tree.

Giles, Bourhis, and Taylor (1977) discuss language shift from the perspective of language maintenance. They present three factors as greatly influencing language maintenance: status, demographics, and institutional support which they combine into the language characteristic "ethnolinguistic vitality".

Language spread

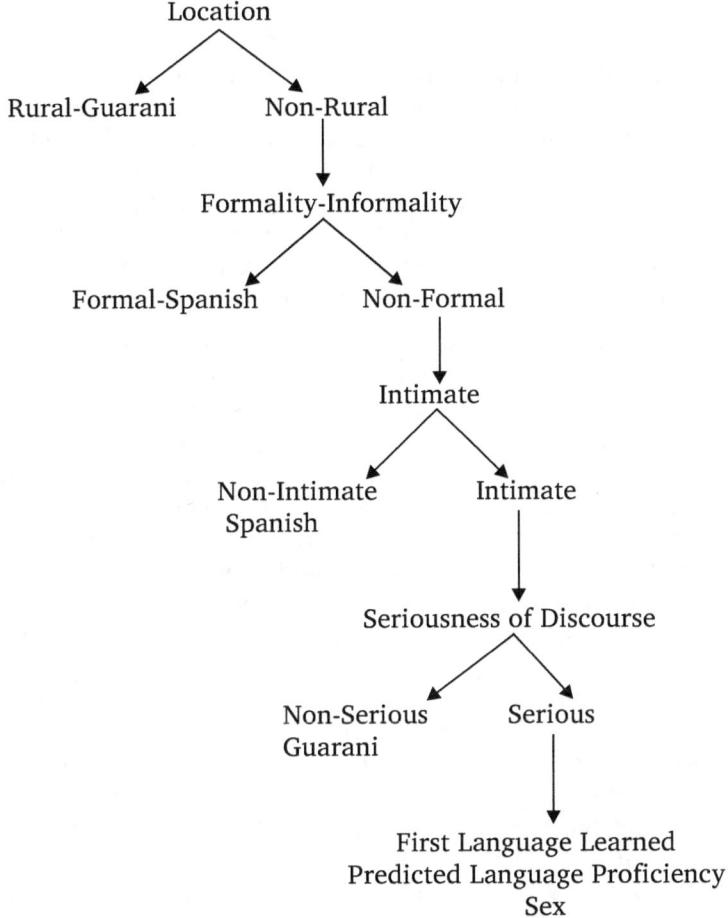

Figure 2.1 Ruben's decision-making tree (1968:526)

Susan Gal (1979) reports on a study that she carried out in Oberwart, on the Hungarian-Austrian border. Her study involved the shift from Hungarian to German. Concerning which language is claimed to be spoken by the population of Oberwart, she states, "Most important, for a certain set of bilingual speakers, neither status is claimed all of the time, and neither language is used invariably" (1979:172).

She goes on to say,

> The distribution of conversational language-switching among Oberwart bilinguals show that it is not characteristic of all

> speakers nor of all the interactions of any one speaker. Rather, it is historically and contextually limited. This, in fact, is part of its importance. Viewed not in isolation but as part of the community-wide process of language shift, conversational language-switching can be explained as the middle and variable step in the process by which the language choice patterns of the community change from categorical use of one language to categorical use of the other. It occurs in contexts where the old form is no longer invariably used, and the new form is not yet invariably used. (Gal 1979:173)

I propose that in the study of the dynamics of language shift or spread, it is this "middle and variable step" that is of the most interest. It is for this reason that I project studying language shift from the variable, individual perspective, i.e., the agglomerate of choices made by individuals.

Bourdieu and Boltanski (1975) present a model of language use and language shift which is based on what they call the *marché linguistique*. In this model, people "buy" by investing time to know a language well, or to know the prestige dialect as it should be spoken (legitimized language), and "sell" by using language, which has become a commodity. The proper use of language brings about profit in showing distinctiveness, authority, and symbolic power.

Haugen holds a similar view in his "ecology of language". People buy into a language by learning it and then benefit from the use of that language. He uses the term "language market" to refer to this buying and benefiting process, and recommends that dying languages be protected, as an endangered species is protected, thus adding a type of subsidization to the language market theory.

Bourdieu (1982) compares language to a treasure and people to store houses, each holding different amounts of the treasure. This treasure is acquired through diligence at school or study and is used to establish and maintain social standing, demand deference, and to augment the chances of one's words being effective. He explains that the effectiveness of a discourse often depends on the perceptions that the audience has of the speaker. He holds that the style and quality of the language used proclaims the authority and social competence of the speaker, much in the same way a uniform, or a degree, or a speaking platform and microphone would proclaim the authority and social competence of a speaker.

Thus, I surmise that for Bourdieu, the dynamic behind language shift is the desire to acquire and use a language which would bring about distinction, respect, authority, and the appearance of competence. There would be the buying of the linguistic commodity by acquiring the spreading language, and the spending of the commodity by its use, hoping to bring about gain. Assuming the correctness of this surmise, it is noteworthy that Bourdieu approaches the dynamics of language shift and language change from the perspective of individuals being motivated and seeking their own good, and not from the perspective of changes on the community level.

In 1978, David Sankoff and Suzanne Laberge constructed an index of economic activity within the linguistic market theory in order to statistically verify the legitimacy of the theory. They used a subjective type of measurement, where professional and graduate students in sociolinguistics rated 120 speakers on "the relative importance of the legitimized language in the socioeconomic life of the speaker" (1978:241). These ratings were assigned a numeric value and combined for each speaker, giving an index of participation in the linguistic market for each speaker.

The speakers chosen for this evaluation were individual subjects in the Montreal French corpus, and thus details of their linguistic behavior were available. For each speaker there was a measure available of the use of *être* as auxiliary, a measure of the use of *ce que* to head embedded constructions, and a measure of the use of *on* instead of *ils* for the first person plural pronoun when the referent does not include the speaker or the hearer.

Using a maximum likelihood program, they found that in each of the variables discussed *(être, ce que, on)*, "the index of participation in the linguistic market was by far the most important explanatory variable as measured by the significance of the difference in log likelihood" (1978:246). The next most important explanatory variable was education.

The strength of the index of participation in the linguistic market in explaining or predicting the use of certain variants of sociolinguistic variables statistically verifies the relevancy of the linguistic market theory. Saukoff and Laberge conclude that individuals make language choices based on what they perceive to be their own benefit.

Liberson (1982) presents a system of factors that cause language spread that are based on the community perspective. He observes that the factors involved in the beginning of language spread are not always those that are pertinent in the continuation of the spread.

Fasold (1984) maintains that certain factors are very pertinent in explaining and predicting language shift. These factors include: industrialization, urbanization, migration, proletarianization, and government policies pre- and proscribing language use in education and other government institutions. Nevertheless, he holds that there has been "very little success in using any combination of [these factors] to predict when language shift will occur" (Fasold 1984:217). In general, Fasold maintains that there is a strong consensus that "we do not know how to predict shift."

Grosjean (1982) itemizes numerous factors that play a role in code choice such as participants, situation, content of discourse, and formation of interaction. He also holds that multiple factors are usually involved in language choice, with different factors having different weights. Grosjean's factors, unlike those given by Fasold, are not based on the community at large, or the society, but for the most part, on the participants and the speech situation.

The same can be said for Hymes' (1974) relevant factors for code choice: situation, genre, participants, and act-sequence which are primarily based on the participants and the speech situation.

In the literature, much of the discussion concerning code choice focuses on individuals and the speech situation, while much of the discussion concerning language shift focuses on the community or even nation. This is natural in that code choice is a function of individuals and language shift is a function of societies.

However, I believe that this societal perspective in language shift discussion has been detrimental to a more complete understanding of language shift. Shift occurs when code choices are individually motivated to go in a certain direction. The motivating factors are influenced by the society, but they are most often pertinent in relation to the perceived good of the speaker.

In 1985, John Edwards attributes code choice, and ultimately language shift, to "pragmatic decisions in which another variety is seen as more important for the future" (1985:71). He holds that different pragmatic considerations such as power, social access, and material advancement are of supreme importance in the study of language use and shift patterns and are the major determinants of success in any language-planning activity.

Edwards also notes, "History shows that language shift is the rule, not the exception" (1985:96). He maintains that ethnic identity often survives language loss, and that the best predictor of language shift is the past language-shift history of the speech community. Edwards concludes that the only way to influence language shift is to alter the entire social fabric of the language community.

Wardhaugh (1987) attributes the dynamics of language spread, at least partially, to factors which have to do with language attractiveness to individual speakers, factors which are mostly below the level of consciousness of the speakers. His discussion of such factors is not written from an individual motivation perspective, but rather from a community, or even a national perspective.

In 1992, Fase, Jaspaert, and Kroon note that the language loss process is closely related to the language shift process, and "if individuals lose the ability to use their own language, they will automatically shift towards other means of expression" (1992:9–10). I agree that language loss is closely related to language shift; however, I think that the above stated approach that language loss causes or contributes to language shift is backwards thinking. Language shift contributes to language loss, not the other way around.

Pandharipande (1992:253) presents four perspectives from which language shift has been examined by scholars:

1. the functional motivations for and social correlates of language shift.[2]
2. language shift as a process of language change.[3]
3. the psychological dimension of language shift.[4]
4. the impact of education and language planning/policy on language shift.[5]

He states that all of these perspectives are focusing "entirely on the functional aspect of shift" (1992:253) and are basically ignoring other important areas such as formal structure aspects of language shift, the effects of shift on the target language, and the relationship between language shift and language loss. He concludes, "language shift leads to emergence of variation not only in the shifting language but also in the target language" (1992:254). This conclusion seems a bit simplistic in that he appears to be making a universal statement, and does not allow for differences in the number of speakers between the languages involved.

Thomason and Kaufman (1991) also talk about the impact of shift on the target language, but limit the influence of shift on the target language to cases where the shift occurs rapidly and the shifting population is very large in relation to the mother tongue speakers of the target language.

Don Kulick notes, "The most widely read monographs on language shift all make heavy use of participant observation as a means of gathering and evaluating data on shift" (1992:9). He holds that language shift is caused by "shifts in personal and group values and goals" (1992:9), and that the key to understanding language shift is understanding how people view and manipulate their conceptions of themselves and of the world around them. This perspective leaves out the important step of how societal values are interpreted, manifested, and even formed and would bring one to

---

[2]Giles et al. 1979; Gumperz 1966; Schach 1980.
[3]Bailey 1973; Bickerton 1973; Fasold 1984; Gal 1979; Gumperz 1971; Labov 1972; Sankoff 1977.
[4]Veltman 1983; Jones 1981; Liberson 1965.
[5]Cobarrubias and Fishman 1983.

the conclusion that personal motivations are at the heart of an understanding of language shift.[6]

This overview of some of the writings on language shift indicates that there is a long tradition of respect for the individual in the process, which views language shift as the result of individually motivated choices, with the motivations tied in to societal values. Also, financial and social motivations surface often in the discussion. It is evident, too, that those who approached language shift from the individual motivation perspective, in general, were much less pessimistic about the current state of the field than those who approached language shift from a macrosocietal level.

---

[6]See Kulick's case study of language shift of children in Papua New Guinea from Gapun to Tok Pisin (1992:20).

3
Quantitative Approach Orientation

Language shift has often been studied through participant observation of a society and through speculations about whole societies. To my knowledge, language shift patterns have never before been quantitatively studied. As the quantitative approach has brought immense insights to the area of language change, i.e., the normal, language-internal change-over-time process, it is hoped that a quantitative study of language shift will bring insight to the understanding of language shift.

Labov (1965) demonstrates how individuals' choice of language-internal speech style is influenced by many different factors. Among these factors are participants in the conversation, location, degree of formality, and the social motivations and aspirations of the speaker. Central to this perspective is the variability of normal speech (a certain situation might call for a particular speech variant a certain percentage of the time).

The hypothesis presented in Weinreic, Labov, and Herzog (1968) is that all change involves variation, but that there is much variation present without change, thus, variability can be the synchronic manifestation of diachronic language change. This hypothesis has been verified in the areas of phonology, syntax, and lexical semantic change (Gal 1978).

Even as societal language change patterns were profitably studied from the perspective of individuals' variable behavior, I maintain that language choice can also profitably be explored from a viewpoint of individuals' variable behavior. As in the case of language change, where a society does not change their speech in a uniform block, neither does language shift occur among the members of a population in a uniform block. Societal patterns are modified by change being introduced by individuals or subgroups.

Susan Gal (1978) proposes the idea that language shift also has its source in synchronic variation, and can profitably be studied through synchronic variation. She states:

> Linguistic change is neither so fast nor so slow as to be unobservable; new forms which eventually replace older forms can first be located in synchronic variants in the speech of subgroups within the community; and changes observed over time are the result of the redistribution of synchronic variants to different linguistic environments, to different social situations, and to different speakers...language use, or more specifically, the pattern of language choice in a bilingual community, also undergoes change according to these same general principles. (1978:227)

Gal demonstrates how in Oberwart, an Austrian community which was bilingual in Hungarian and German, the choice of language was used not only to show a solidarity and identification with either the Hungarian speaking agricultural population or the German speaking industrial population, but was also used for "expressing the kind of rhetorical stylistic meanings which had previously been communicated through variation within each language" (1978:228).

A code switching from Hungarian to German was used when the speaker wanted to have a "'topper' in a disagreement; a last word which is not outdone and which serves to win the argument", or to "strengthen commands and to assert expertise and authoritativeness about an issue or about a technical specialty" (Gal 1978:236). She later states: "Opinions and judgments appear to gain credibility and stature when uttered in German, the language associated by Oberwarters with work, knowledge of the world beyond home, and therefore sophistication" (1978:236). This rhetorical stylistic use of switching from one language to another is similar to a style shift to a prestigious style, which often can have the same type of authoritative impact.

In her 1979 work, also on the shift from Hungarian to German in Oberwart, Gal maintains that the choice of which language to choose from one's personal inventory is similar to the choice of which speech style to use in a monolingual setting. She states:

> In particular, when phonological changes are a result of speakers' conscious attempts to alter their speech in the direction of a prestige form—as is the case in Oberwart—then, in the course of phonological change: "The linguistic variable...shows regular stylistic stratification as well as social stratification

(Labov 1965:535)." In short, here too, expression of social identity and expression of other communicative functions are accomplished by the same variable linguistic means. In these respects the social mechanism of change between two languages is the same as the mechanism of change within a single language. (1979:174)

Thus for Gal, language shift, similar to phonological or syntactic or lexical change, can be synchronically observed in the alternation between old and new forms, and in the spreading of the old/new variation to new speakers, new styles and levels of formality, and new domains of speech. Similar to phonological, syntactic, and lexical change, the moving force behind language shift is supplied by the social rhetorical meanings associated with the alternate forms.

There are many other similarities between language spread and language change. In both, women are usually in the forefront of the innovation. Age plays a major role in the distribution of the innovation. Prestige factors are of paramount importance in both spread and change. And motivations for the innovations appear to mirror each other. Both language spread and language change involve choices, be it of code or variety or style; choices are made based on motivations that are very possibly identical.

Gumperz, maintains that multilingual members of a multilingual society choose between languages in a similar way that monolinguals choose between language styles. He states that bilinguals:

> ...alternate among languages for much the same reasons that monolinguals select among styles of a single language (Rubin 1961; Fishman 1965). That is to say, the same social pressures which would lead a monolingual to change from colloquial to formal or technical styles may induce a bilingual to shift from one language to another. Where this is the case, the differences between monolingual and bilingual behavior thus lies in the linguistic coding of socially equivalent processes. In one instance speakers select among lexical or phonetic variants of what they regard as the same language; in the other case, speakers choose between what they view as two linguistic entities. (Gumperz and Wilson 1971:230–231)

In this way, Gumperz calls style shifting and code choice "socially equivalent processes". Because of the central role that code choice plays in language shift, and because of the central role that style shifting plays in language change, choice (of code or style) can be seen as a factor that associates the processes of language shift and language change.

Fasold (1984) also relates the process of choice between codes and the choice between variants in one language, stating that the "kinds of choices cannot be cleanly separated from each other" (1984:181). Sociolinguistic variation, as seen by Fasold, covers both choices between codes and choices between variants in one language.

> Sociolinguistic variation implies that speakers have a choice among language varieties. This choice may be between one language or another, depending on the situation (code-switching), whether or not to use elements from one language while speaking another (code-mixing), or among the myriad variants within a single-language system. (1984:208)

As discussed in chapter 2, Bourdieu's (1982) linguistic market view of language shift does not make a hard distinction between transaction choices that involve different codes and those involving different styles within one code. He also leans heavily toward a dynamic that involves individuals who are seeking their own good and making decisions and choices of variants which are characterized by different social rhetorical meanings. Bourdieu unites the concepts of language change and language shift as similar types of processes in the linguistic market, and relies on a view of the dynamic of both language change and language shift that is based on insights drawn from individuals.

John Edwards (1985:50) states, "Language shift often reflects pragmatic desires for social mobility and an improved standard of living." Normally, social mobility and improvements in the standard of living are phenomena that work on the individual or family level and not on the community or society level. Edwards also states, "We note again a powerful concern for linguistic practicality, communicative efficiency, social mobility, and economic advancement" (1985:85). All these concerns operate basically on the individual level.

There have been numerous parallels drawn between language shift and language change, and importantly, numerous parallels that imply viewing this process from the perspective of the individual. As quantitative studies of language change quantify and study how individuals behave in society, quantitative studies of language shift should also focus on how individuals behave in society. This emphasis on the individual is in no way a denial of the societal domain of shift, and in no way implies a homogeneity of all the members of a society; it is simply a research tool in studying language shift. In the same way that measuring the formants of individuals' vowels is a research tool in studying language change, studying individuals' patterns and motivations of language choice is a research tool in studying language shift. Such patterns of choice, whether between variants of a sociolingistic variable in one language, or between codes in a multilingual situation, must be interpreted in light of the patterns of choices in the whole community.

With the above in consideration, I prefer to view shift in community language use patterns as a result of the agglomerate of choices made by individuals. Language spread is thus best studied from the perspective of individuals' choices and motivations.

In general, my study of the Sango data presented in this work, as well as readings and studies in the area of language shift, has led me to the following consideration: Languages spread, shift occurs, because individuals make decisions to use certain languages in certain situations. These individual decisions are motivated by what each individual considers their personal good. People exploit and expand their linguistic repertoires in order to gain personal benefit. When language spread or shift occurs, it is occurring because people are choosing to speak a different language for their own perceived benefit. Language shift does not "happen" to a community, rather a community makes shift happen through individual choices motivated by a search for personal good.

When this is happening, all the members of a community are not behaving homogeneously, acting in tandem. Different individuals and different subsections of the community are behaving differently from others. Patterns of the social distribution of those acting in similar ways will be evident. We expect and find strong correlations between different social factors and code-choice behaviors. Only the synthesis of how all the members of the community are behaving gives a complete picture of the language shift situation.

With the study of sound change, the dependent variable with which the independent variables of social factors interact, is often a subject's percentage of use of one variant of a linguistic variable. In studying language spread, an effective dependent variable is the subjects' proficiency in the language that is spreading. It is in reference to this dependent variable that independent variables of social factors can be studied.

In sound change, a speaker using a higher percentage of the variants that were in the direction of change would be seen as being on the forefront of sound change. In language spread, a speaker who is more proficient in the spreading language would be seen as one who is on the forefront of language shift. For this reason, the primary measure for each subject should be one of proficiency in the spreading language. This is assuming that there is a tight relationship between frequency of use of a language and proficiency in that language. In the context of the spread of a nonprimary language, I would maintain that this is a safe assumption, especially in the Central African context where gaining proficiency in different languages is a social expectation.

It has been demonstrated that an individual's choice of speech style is influenced by many different factors. Among these factors are participants in the conversation, location, degree of formality, and the social motivations and aspirations of the speaker. I propose that these same factors can and do influence the choice of language in multilingual situations in the same ways that they influence the choice of speech styles in monolingual settings.

If indeed there are great similarities between language change and language shift, we can expect great similarities in the distribution of the social factors that predict them: factors such as age, schooling, social class, attention paid to speech, sex, audience, and rural/urban considerations. As will be seen in the following chapters, there are indeed these great similarities, giving further reason to feel secure in the association of language shift and language change.

4
Sentence Repetition Tests (SRTs)

The second language proficiency testing device used in the study of the spread of bilingualism in Sango is the SENTENCE REPETITION TEST (SRT) (Radloff 1991). SRT testing is based on short-term memory restrictions. Subjects are asked to repeat a series of increasingly complex sentences in the language being tested. The premise of the SRT is that people's ability to repeat these sentences will reflect their proficiency in the language in question.

This premise is based on limitations of short term memory. If a subject is not familiar with the language for which he or she is being tested, he or she will only be able to remember about seven sounds or phones (seven being an average standard limit of short term memory). If the subject is more familiar with the language, he or she would be able to remember and reproduce about seven syllables. If the subject is even more familiar with the language, he or she would be able to identify, remember, and reproduce about seven words. Even greater familiarity with the language would allow the subject to repeat around seven clauses or phrases. This assumes that it is easier to remember sounds than syllables, syllables than words, and so on.

Memory tests were first developed and used as a device to test not language proficiency, but mental ability. In the 1960s, the use of the memory test was expanded to test whether or not certain constructions were already in the grammar of young subjects and to examine cross-dialectal patterns. In a study of Afro-American Vernacular English (AAVE), memory tests were used to investigate adolescents' control of morphological and syntactic patterns (Labov, et. al 1968:310–334). The tests showed that where there was a difference between standard English and AAVE, and where the AAVE pattern was categorical, the subjects, when asked to repeat a standard English sentence, would replace the standard English patterns with the AAVE patterns. Where the AAVE pattern was variable, the subjects would repeat verbatim the standard English sentences.

Labov et al. (1968:312) state, "what was most impressive was the way in which certain SE [Standard English] sentences were understood and repeated back instantly in AAVE form—a process of considerable significance for linguistic theory." For example, in embedded yes-no questions, AAVE has the pattern of retaining inverted word order without a complementizer. Below is one of the sentences in their first test, along with two examples of how the sentence was repeated, maintaining inverted word order without the complementizer.

SE-7: I asked Alvin if he knows how to play basketball.
Boot: I ax Alvin do he know how to play basketball.
Money: I ax Alvin if—do he know how to play basketball.
(Labov, Cohen, Robins, and Lewis: 1968:314)

Baratz (1969) used a memory test to demonstrate substantial differences between the grammars of white and black children. She made up a test of fifteen standard English sentences and fifteen nonstandard English sentences. Using random ordering of the sentences, she had thirty black and thirty white third and fifth graders repeat the phrases. The blacks did significantly better than the whites in repeating the nonstandard sentences. And the whites did significantly better than the blacks in repeating the standard sentences.

Lado proposed the following tentative conclusions concerning memory span. (Memory Span is "the length of a series of verbal forms that can be reproduced immediately after a single exposure" [Lado 1965:124].)

1. Memory span is shorter in a foreign language than in the native language.
2. Memory span in a foreign language increases with mastery of the language.
3. The difference between the native and the foreign language memory span is greater when the material in the foreign language contains the pronunciation and grammatical contrasts between the languages.
4. The relation of memory span to foreign language learning is greater for contextual material than for digits.
5. Memory span cannot be used as the only criterion of proficiency in a foreign language, but it is a factor or dimension of knowing a foreign language.

6. Information on memory span should probably be taken into account in deciding the length of oral practice sentences in pedagogical materials. (Lado 1965:128–129)

These tentative conclusions enabled others to use memory span tests to evaluate language proficiency. Natalicio (1967:107) argues that "successful sentence repetition involves language processing, not the mere mimicry of syllables." Harris (1970:203) investigated using group-administered memory span tests. He concluded that "performance on the experimental test correlated quite highly (from .73 to .79) with performance on standardized listening and grammar tests." He also found that "the difficulty of the test sentences appeared to be determined very largely by their length and syntactical complexity" (1970:203).

Scheibner-Herzig, Sauerbrey, and Kokoschka (1991:229) state, "repetition of a sentence is not a trivial or superficial task but one that involves listening comprehension, memory, and reproduction."

Carla F. Radloff (1991), along with Dan Hallberg, David Marshall, and Charles Meeker, developed the sentence repetition test (SRT). The SRT is a language proficiency testing device based on verbatim repetition of sentences. When the SRT is given along with a different measure of language competence, the results of the two measures regularly correlate highly, thus the SRT is seen as an accurate language proficiency testing device. It is also easy to administer to large groups. The correlation between the SRT and interview style language proficiency measures is very high.

Fasold (1984:104) presents the following, which he calls a typical interpretation system for the coefficient of correlation.

Table 4.1 Interpretation of coefficient of correlation

```
0.01–0.20  slight, almost negligible relationship
0.20–0.40  low correlation; definite but small relationship
0.40–0.70  moderate correlation; substantial relationship
0.70–0.90  high correlation; marked relationship
0.90–0.99  very high correlation; very dependable relationship
```

However, the coefficient of correlation is only reliable, and should only be used when the data exhibit a linear relationship with homogeneous variance. The coefficient of correlation is a measure of linear relationship. In order to determine if the coefficient of correlation can be used, the standard procedure is to chart out the data in a scattergram (one testing measure against the other), and to see if the distribution of the data is linear and if it seems to have homogeneous variance. Linearity is determined by whether the pattern of the distribution of the points follow a straight line. Figure 4.1 illustrates linearity, figure 4.2 does not.

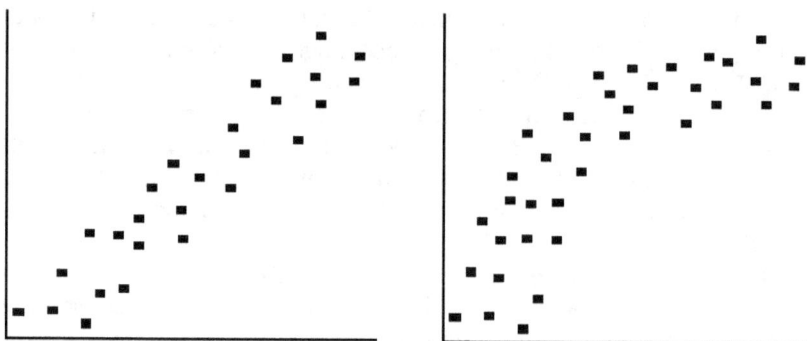

Figure 4.1 Linearity   Figure 4.2 Non-linearity

Homogeneity of variance can be assumed if the pattern of distribution of the points is not different at different parts of the linear relationship. The grouping of the points is just as tight at the bottom of the chart as it is in the middle of the chart and as it is at the top of the chart when the variance is homogeneous. Figure 4.3 illustrates a linear relationship with homogeneous variance. Figure 4.4 illustrates a linear relationship, but with heterogeneous variance.

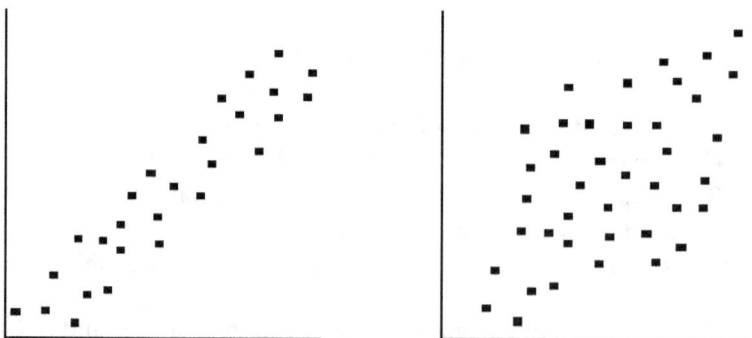

Figure 4.3 Homogeneous variance   Figure 4.4 Heterogeneous variance

In chapter 5, I make use of the coefficient of correlation between the SRT and an independent testing device to compare modification of the SRT to the original SRT as presented by Radloff. If the modified SRT produces a higher coefficient of correlation with the independent testing device than does the unmodified SRT, the modification will be deemed an improvement.

The development of the Sango SRT basically followed the method presented in Radloff (1991:37–75). Divergences from and modifications to her method are presented and discussed in the next chapter.

The first phase of the work was to select fifty to sixty sentences to be used in the initial form of the SRT. These sentences needed to be examples of natural, spoken speech. They also needed to differ in length and complexity. The goal was to have fifty to sixty sentences which ranged in difficulty and length, from the very short and simple to the very long and complex.

During the phase of the selection of the initial fifty to sixty sentences, I worked with Jérôme Sitamon, Gaston Dobi, and Christian Dagnan. Certain sentences were extracted from recorded samples of speech. Others were formed at that time.

For the sentences which needed to be longer and more complex, care was taken to assure a diversity of different grammatical structures, such as dependent clauses and embedded clauses. A wide variety of content in the sentences was also desired. Different descriptions and action sentences were selected. However, questions were avoided because subjects would desire to answer questions instead of simply repeating the sentences, and we wanted to keep subjects focused on the repetition task per se. Sentences which could be interpreted as political or controversial were also excluded.

The sentences were transcribed, and glosses in French were interlinearized. A free translation in French was added. The sentences were then arranged in order of suspected difficulty. Shorter sentences were placed before longer sentences. For sentences of the same length, sentences that were less complex grammatically or which had more common vocabulary items were placed before sentences that were more complex grammatically or which had less common vocabulary. The sentences were then numbered and recorded (along with their numbers) in this easy-to-difficult order. Pauses of about three seconds were left between each sentence. Even the sentences which were derived from recorded speech samples were re-recorded so that they would be in the same speech style and of the same recording quality as the other sentences.

The recorded sentences were played for various mother tongue speakers of Sango, who were asked to comment on which sentences did not sound natural. Those identified as not sounding natural were eliminated. As good language skills are highly valued and the concept of naturalness in language is well-understood among educated Sango speakers, these steps largely excluded non-natural sounding sentences.

The recorded sentences were then played for other educated mother tongue speakers of Sango, who were instructed to repeat the sentences verbatim. The pause button of the tape recorder was pushed after each sentence to provide the necessary time for the repetition. A dual headphone setup was used to provide high quality audio reproduction of the taped sentences.

Sentences which were too long or too complex to be repeated by educated mother tongue speakers of Sango were eliminated. However, sentences which were difficult to repeat for these educated mother tongue speakers of Sango, but which still could be repeated without error by some of the speakers, were kept in order to distinguish the ability of more advanced speakers.

The sentences which remained, forty-five in number, were then re-recorded in the same easy-to-hard order. Care was taken to assure that the recording was as high a quality as possible. A Marantz cassette tape recorder with manual recording level, a recording level meter, and an external dynamic microphone was used. A recording location with a low level of background noise was selected. The actual location was an inner courtyard of the abandoned palace of ex-Emperor Bokassa. Recording conditions were very good. The outdoor area was surrounded by the deserted palace buildings, and there was no noise from wind, nor was there any unwanted resonance or echoing from a ceiling. The sentences were spoken by Christian Dagnan and recorded without any numbering and with a three second pause between each sentence.

The next step was to select fifty subjects for a repetition test of these forty-five sentences. They had already been tested with a different Sango proficiency measure—the Reported Proficiency Evaluation (RPE) from Radloff (1991:47).

The RPE is an estimation of proficiency in a language where subjects are evaluated by educated, mother tongue speakers of that language who are in regular contact with those being evaluated. Radloff (1991:127–153) provides a description of the evaluation and its application.

In administering the RPE, mother tongue speakers of Sango are sought to supply RPE evaluations of Sango speakers of differing abilities with whom they are in daily contact. Because of the high level of contact between those doing the evaluation, and those being evaluated, the evaluators could work from their memory of the ability of those they were evaluating. This evaluation could not be done in Bangui, the capitol of the country because, although there were very many educated mother tongue speakers of Sango, there were very few people who did not speak Sango well. For this reason, the RPE rating at this stage of the SRT development process took place in Bossangoa, a large town in the north of the country.

In Bossangoa, seven mother tongue speakers of Sango each evaluated about five of their acquaintances. The mother tongue speakers (MTS), who were mostly high school teachers, were first asked to study a series of paragraphs that described differing levels of competence in the area of accent, adapted from Radloff (1991:147), and listed in the order of poor to good.

a. Pronunciation frequently unintelligible: Because his pronunciation is very bad, people often cannot even understand his speech.
b. Frequent gross errors and a very heavy accent make understanding difficult, require frequent repetition: Because of frequent big errors in pronunciation and a very heavy accent, it is difficult for people to understand him. People time and again ask him to repeat himself.
c. "Foreign accent" requires concentrated listening and mispronunciations lead to occasional misunderstanding and apparent errors in grammar or vocabulary: People must listen carefully to understand him because he speaks the test language with a vernacular accent. Sometimes his mispronunciation makes people not understand or think he used the wrong word or bad grammar, but really it was only his poor pronunciation.
d. Marked "foreign accent" and occasional mispronunciations which do not interfere with understanding: People can easily understand his speaking, even with his pronunciation errors. People can easily tell from his accent that the test language is not his mother tongue.
e. No conspicuous mispronunciations, but would not be taken for a native speaker: Even though there is no obvious error in his pronunciation, people still do not consider him a mother-tongue speaker of the test language because of his slight accent.
f. Native pronunciation, with no trace of "foreign accent": His pronunciation and accent are so good that you would think that the test language is his mother tongue.

Because the RPE evaluators were all proficient in French, French being the language of instruction in the Central African Republic, the Accent Proficiency Description was presented to them in French, as were the proficiency descriptions for the other areas. The RPE uses proficiency descriptions in five different areas: accent, grammar, vocabulary, fluency, and comprehension. For each area, there is a set of paragraphs like the sample one for accent above. For each set of paragraphs, paragraph (a) corresponds to minimal proficiency, paragraph (f) corresponds to native speaker proficiency, and the other paragraphs (b–e) correspond to augmenting gradations between (a) and (f).

An RPE evaluator is first asked to identify five or six speakers of Sango that he or she would evaluate, and who will later be tested by the Sango SRT. The evaluator is then asked to study the paragraph set pertaining to accent proficiency. She or he is then asked to identify the speaker, among his five or six, who has the best accent. He or she is then asked to identify the speaker who has the worst or heaviest accent. A set of small cards was prepared with the name of each one of the people being evaluated on a separate card. When the evaluator identified the speaker with the best accent, the card for that speaker was placed far from the evaluator on the desk space in front of the evaluator. The card for the speaker that was identified as having the worst accent was placed close to the evaluator on the desk.

The evaluator was then asked to identify who, among the remaining three or four people, had the best accent. The card for the person thus identified was placed next to the card of the speaker who had the best accent, in line with the other card on the table. The evaluator was then asked to identify who among those still remaining had the worst accent. That person's card was placed next to the card of the person having the worst accent, in line with the other cards on the table.

This procedure was repeated until all of the cards were on the table, in a line, with the cards of those having the progressively higher proficiencies further away from the evaluator. This ranking of the accent proficiencies of these speakers was then verified by asking the evaluator if A or B had the better accent, if B or C had the better accent, if C or D had the better accent, and so on.

The evaluator was then asked to select, from the paragraphs describing accent proficiency, the paragraph that best described the accent of the speaker he had ranked as having the best accent. I recorded this response on a response sheet. Next, the evaluator was asked to select the paragraph that best described the accent of the speaker he had ranked as having the worst accent. Then a paragraph was selected for the speaker he had ranked as second best in accent, then a paragraph for the speaker he had ranked as second worst, and so on until a paragraph was ascribed to describe the accent of all of the people being evaluated.

In the cases where the evaluator had difficulty deciding which of two adjacent paragraphs best described the accent of a particular speaker, I recorded an intermediary level, between the two paragraphs.

In the rare cases where the ascription of the paragraphs contradicted the previous ranking of the speakers, I would then return to the ranking of the subjects to see where the problem occurred. In most if not all cases, the evaluator had changed his mind about the ranking of certain speakers, in light of the ascription of the descriptive paragraphs.

A numerical value was then ascribed to each speaker to represent his or her accent proficiency. This numerical value was determined by reference to the scale set up by the Educational Testing Services (ETS). ETS had established the scale to help evaluate bilingualism in Peace Corps and Foreign Service activities. Educational Testing Services (1970) gave the following numerical values to similar descriptive paragraphs:

Proficiency description	A	B	C	D	E	F
Accent	0	1	2	2	3	4

The next step for the evaluators was to repeat all of the above procedure, but this time for the grammar aspect of proficiency. After the grammar, came the vocabulary aspect, then the fluency aspect, then the comprehension aspect of proficiency. For each aspect, the evaluators first ranked the speakers, then ascribed to them a descriptive paragraph. I then ascribed a point value to the paragraph chosen for each speaker and each competence aspect according to the following scale (Educational Testing Services 1970).

Table 4.2 RPE point values for proficiency descriptions

Proficiency description	A	B	C	D	E	F
Accent	0	1	2	2	3	4
Grammar	6	12	18	24	30	36
Vocabulary	4	8	12	16	20	24
Proficiency description	A	B	C	D	E	F
Fluency	2	4	6	8	10	12
Comprehension	4	8	12	15	19	23

The total of each speaker's scores, combining the number for the appropriate paragraph in the accent section, the appropriate paragraph in the grammar section, etc., would then be the RPE score.

The RPE score was then converted to a standard second language proficiency level by using the following table (Educational Testing Service:1970).

Table 4.3 Second language proficiency levels and RPE scores

Total	16–25	26–32	33–42	43–52	53–62	63–72	73–82	83–92	93–99
Level	0+	1	1+	2	2+	3	3+	4	4+

After these subjects had been tested with the SRT and evaluated with the RPE, the next step was a comparison of the results of the two measures, to see what degree of correlation existed. Figure 4.5 is a scattergram of the SRT long form calibrated against the results of the RPE. The coefficient of correlation that exists is $r = .673$ (Multiple R), a moderate to high correlation.

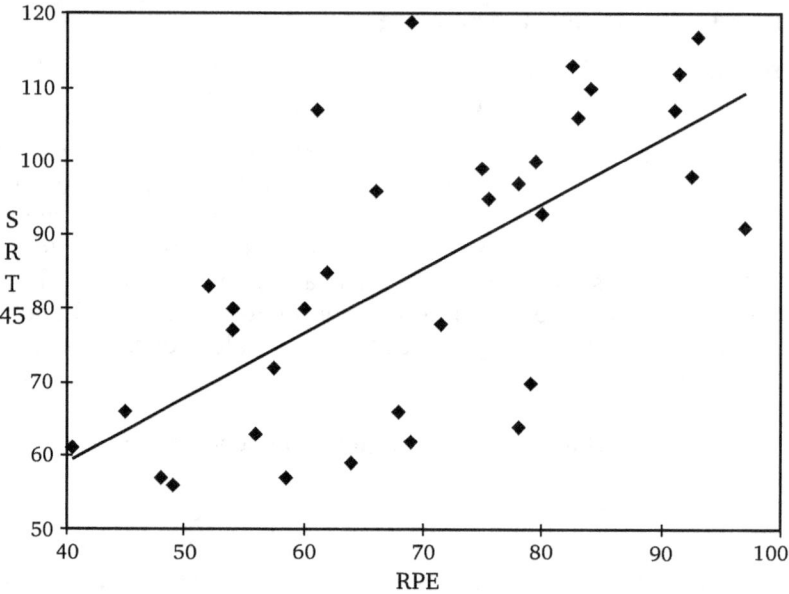

Figure 4.5 Scattergram SRT long form and RPE

The next step in Radloff's recommended procedure is the selection of the fifteen sentences that best indicate language proficiency when used in the short form of the SRT. The short form is the one that is used for the widespread testing of second language proficiency among a large sample of a population. It is limited to fifteen sentences in order to limit the time of application of the test to each individual subject.

The sentences selected for the short form of the SRT should "represent the full range of difficulty levels" (Radloff 1991:60). The sentences should also be the ones "which best distinguish speakers with respect to their second-language proficiency" (Radloff 1991:54).

In order to select sentences which come from all areas of the difficulty spectrum, Radloff used an index that she calls the "difficulty level". The difficulty level is calibrated for each of the forty-five sentences in the long form of the SRT by calculating the total points attained for that sentence by all of the subjects and dividing that number by the number of possible points. In the case of the Sango SRT, there were thirty-five subjects who took the long form, thus the total number of points that were scored on a particular sentence was divided by 105 (35 x 3 possible points). Radloff (1991:59–60) recommends subtracting this number from 1 in order to come up with a number between 0 and 1 where the higher the number, the more difficult the sentence.

As an example of the difficulty level, if the total points for sentence 24 (for all 35 subjects) were totaled and the sum was 91, this 91 is divided by 105 (the number of subjects times 3 possible points) giving .87. This .87 is then subtracted from 1 giving the difficulty level index of .13.

The difficulty level is a simple and effective index of the difficulty that the SRT long-form subjects had with individual sentences. A low number indicates that they had little trouble with the sentence, and a high number indicates that they had more trouble. The difficulty level index is thus useful in selecting sentences for the final form of the SRT which reflect the full range of difficulty.

In order to select the sentences "which best distinguish speakers with respect to their second-language proficiency", Radloff (1991:54) uses an index which she calls the discrimination index. This index indicates which sentences are better suited to predicting how well subjects perform on the SRT.

To arrive at this discrimination index, Radloff relies on a system of rearranging the results of the longer, preliminary SRT, and then applying a procedure which is inspired by the Kendall W correlation coefficient (Radloff 1991:56). She first arranges the data by the total scores of the individual sentences, with the sentences scoring the highest at the top of the data display. Thus, the sentences are displayed from the top to the bottom, the easiest to the hardest. She then arranges the subjects in this data display so that the subjects who scored the highest are displayed in incremental order with the highest scoring subject at the right of the data display. The subjects are displayed, from left to right, with the ones who did the poorest to the ones who did the best. The data display is filled in with the individual results for each subject on each sentence.

Table 4.4 Radloff's hypothetical example of discrimination index calculations (1991:57)

Sent. no.		A	E	I	M	B	F	J	N	C	G	K	O	D	H	L	Sent. Tot.
								Participants									
6.	Actual	1	1	1	2	2	2	2	2	2	2	3	3	3	3	3	32
	Rearr.																
	Diff.																
3.	Actual	0	0	0	1	0	1	1	1	2	2	2	2	2	3	3	20
	Rearr.																
	Diff.																
7.	Actual	0	0	1	0	0	1	1	1	2	2	2	3	2	2	3	20
	Rearr.																
	Diff.																
4.	Actual	0	0	0	0	0	0	1	1	0	3	2	3	3	3	3	19
	Rearr.																
	Diff.																
1.	Actual	0	0	0	0	0	0	1	1	2	3	1	3	3	3	3	17
	Rearr.																
	Diff.																
5.	Actual	0	0	0	0	1	1	1	1	1	1	1	1	2	2	3	15
	Rearr.																
	Diff.																
2.	Actual	0	0	0	0	0	1	1	1	1	1	1	2	2	2	2	14
	Rearr.																
	Diff.																
Subject total score (out of 21)		1	1	2	3	3	6	7	8	9	13	14	15	17	18	20	

After the actual scores on the preliminary form (long form) of the SRT are entered on the data display, these individual scores for each sentence are rearranged on a different line so that all of the 0s are together, all the 1s are together, all the 2s are together, and so on.

The next step in this procedure is to calculate the absolute difference between the individual subject scores for each sentence and the rearranged scores on the data display (see table 4.5). The total of these absolute differences provides the discrimination index for each sentence. A high discrimination index indicates that a sentence did not do a good job in discriminating the results on the total preliminary SRT, and a low discrimination index indicates that a sentence did well.

Table 4.5 Examples of calculations for discrimination index and difficulty level (Radloff 1991:58)

Sent. no.		Participants															Sent Tot.	DL	DL* (Tot. Diff)
		A	E	I	M	B	F	J	N	C	G	K	O	D	H	L			
6.	Actual	1	1	1	2	2	2	2	2	2	2	3	3	3	3	3	32	.29	
	Rearr.	1	1	1	2	2	2	2	2	2	3	3	3	3	3	3			
	Diff.	0	0	0	0	0	0	0	0	0	0	0	0	0	0	0			0
3.	Actual	0	0	0	1	0	1	1	1	2	2	2	2	2	3	3	20	.56	
	Rearr.	0	0	0	0	1	1	1	1	2	2	2	2	2	3	3			
	Diff.	0	0	0	1	1	0	0	0	0	0	0	0	0	0	0			2
7.	Actual	0	0	1	0	0	1	1	1	2	2	2	3	2	2	3	20	.56	
	Rearr.	0	0	0	0	1	1	1	1	2	2	2	2	2	3	3			
	Diff.	0	0	1	0	1	0	0	0	0	0	0	1	0	1	0			4
4.	Actual	0	0	0	0	0	0	1	1	0	3	2	3	3	3	3	19	.58	
	Rearr.	0	0	0	0	0	0	0	1	1	2	3	3	3	3	3			
	Diff.	0	0	0	0	0	0	1	0	1	1	1	0	0	0	0			4
1.	Actual	0	0	0	0	0	0	0	1	1	2	3	1	3	3	3	17	.62	
	Rearr.	0	0	0	0	0	0	1	1	1	2	3	3	3	3	3			
	Diff.	0	0	0	0	0	0	0	0	0	1	1	2	0	0	0			4
5.	Actual	0	0	0	0	1	1	1	1	1	1	1	2	2	3		15	.67	
	Rearr.	0	0	0	0	1	1	1	1	1	1	1	2	2	3				
	Diff.	0	0	0	0	0	0	0	0	0	0	0	0	0	0				0
2.	Actual	0	0	0	0	0	0	1	1	1	1	1	2	2	2	2	14	.69	
	Rearr.	0	0	0	0	0	0	1	1	1	1	1	2	2	2	2			
	Diff.	0	0	0	0	0	0	0	0	0	0	0	0	0	0	0			0
Subject Total score (out of 21)		1	1	2	3	3	6	7	8	9	13	14	15	17	18	20			

*DL = 1.00 − Total/45

Radloff's prescribed method for choosing the sentences to be included in the final form of the SRT uses her difficulty level and discrimination index in the following way. The difficulty level is used to select sentences that represent the full range of difficulty. The discrimination index is used to select sentences that are more discriminating in giving results that match the scores of the preliminary SRT. Thus, sentences with low discrimination index scores are to be chosen (1991:60).

In chapter 5, I discuss where and why I diverged from Radloff's method of choosing the fifteen sentences for the final form of the Sango SRT. In short, I was not comfortable with her discrimination index, designed to show which sentences were best fitted to give the results that the long form of the SRT gave. I felt that a different index would better serve, one that would predict which sentences were suited to giving results that would reflect the level of bilingualism, as shown by the other testing device, the Reported Proficiency Exam (RPE).

The last step recommended by Radloff in the preparation of an SRT is the calculation of the score of the final form, extracted from the results of the longer, preliminary form. Radloff states:

> In order to calibrate the final, fifteen-sentence form of the SRT, an extracted score for each person previously tested is calculated. This is done by removing the rows and sentence totals for the sentences that were not selected for the final set of fifteen. The total score for each subject based on the fifteen sentences that remain is then recalculated. It is assumed that this extracted score represents how the subject would have done had he been given the shortened, final form of the test. (1991:61)

Radloff then recommends using this extracted score to compare with the score of the RPE. She recommends calibrating the SRT through this comparison with the RPE. For this calibration, she discusses three statistics: the line of regression, the standard error of estimate, and the coefficient of correlation.

I am not in agreement with calibrating the SRT against the RPE by using an extracted score from the preliminary SRT. There are too many factors such as subject fatigue and effects of the preceding question that could be involved. I prefer (and I exercised this preference in designing the Sango SRT) testing a new set of subjects with the final form of the SRT (15 sentences) and also with the RPE. It is at this point, with this new set of data, that the SRT can be justly calibrated against the RPE. This calibration provides the basis to predict an Eductional Testing Service type level of language competence from the scores on the SRT.

5

The Development of the Sango SRT

Barrie Wetherill (1992), proposed a number of interesting possibilities for further refinement of Sentence Repetition Testing (SRT). While I was developing the Sango SRT, his propositions inspired me to test some variations on the standard SRT procedure set forth by Carla F. Radloff (1991).

The first variation from the standard procedure was that of using a two-value point system (0 and 1) in scoring the sentence repetitions instead of the four-value point system suggested by Radloff (3 points perfect, no errors in sentence; 2 points one error in sentence; 1 point two errors in sentence, and 0 more than two errors).

The use of a two-value point system was first suggested by Wetherill in conjunction with the inclusion of more sentences in the final form of the SRT. Because of the desire to minimize the administration time required for a single SRT test, I did not consider adding more sentences. I did, however, see profit in investigating the two-value scoring system, comparing it to the four-value system. Some interesting theoretical considerations resulted from this comparison.

The second variation that I investigated was looking at the individual sentence tables of SRT score versus RPE level while the trial is proceeding. This led me to a new factor or index (predictability index) to use in choosing the short form of the SRT, to be used instead of the discrimination index.

As mentioned in chapter 4, I used the coefficient of correlation (product-moment correlation coefficient) quite extensively in this research. If a modification in a measure of language competence resulted in a higher correlation between that measure and another, independent, measure of language competence, I interpreted that higher correlation to imply that the modification was an improvement. In the case of the development of the Sango SRT, where one measure of language competence used was the SRT and the other measure was the RPE, the fact that these measures were so drastically different contributed to the justification of the above interpretation.

The SRT is a test based on short term memory limitations, equating ability to repeat sentences with competence in the language. The RPE is a structured, subjective evaluation performed by qualified people who are in daily contact with those being evaluated. A high correlation between these two measures strongly implies that the two measures are in fact measuring what they are designed to measure, i.e., competence in a language. When one of the measures is modified and the correlation between the two measures increases, this strongly implies that the measures are now doing an even better job in measuring what they are designed to measure. It is in this way that such a modification of the SRT can be deemed an improvement.

When I charted the Sango SRT long form (45 sentences) against the RPE results for the same subjects (see figure 4.5), the relationship appears to be linear and the variance homogeneous. The variance is homogeneous in the sense that there are no apparent differences in the variation present on different parts of the scatter plot. For instance, the degree of clustering in the bottom left of the scatter plot is similar to the degree of clustering in the top right of the scatter plot. The other charts in this research all appear to have the same characteristics. Because the relationships of the measures appears to be linear, and the variance appears to be homogeneous, the coefficient of correlation is an appropriate statistic to use in this research. Thus, the coefficient of correlation is used even to appraise proposed modifications to the standard procedure. If a modification results in a higher correlation between the SRT and the RPE, that modification is seen as desirable. The higher correlations are also reflected in tighter groupings around the regression line on the scatter plots, so the higher correlation can be said to reflect a higher predictability of RPE levels from SRT results.

Two-value scoring systems

The coefficient of correlation of the SRT long form (45 sentences scored with a 0/1/2/3 system) and the RPE was $r = .673$. When I converted all of the SRT individual subjects' sentence scores of 0s, 1s, and 2s to value

"0", and converted all of the 3s to value "1", the correlation with the RPE results was r = .632. This indicated that the four-level scoring system allowed slightly greater predictability of RPE levels from SRT results. The above two-value system gives one point if the sentence was repeated perfectly, and no points if there was any type of mistake.

However, when I used a different type of two-value system, one that gave one point if the response was perfect or if it had only one or two mistakes, and zero points if there were more than two mistakes, the coefficient of correlation (r = .656) was almost as high as that of the four-value scoring system (r = .673). In order to convert the four-value system into this second two-value system, a subject's individual sentence score of 0 received the value "0", while a subject's individual sentence score of 1, 2, or 3, received the value "1".

This same pattern was repeated in the correlations of the shorter SRT (15 sentences) with the RPE. The coefficient of correlation between the short SRT with the four-value scoring system and the RPE was r = .681. The coefficient of correlation between the short SRT with the first two-value scoring system (perfect = 1, not perfect = 0) and the RPE was r = .658. The coefficient of correlation between the short SRT with the second two-value scoring system (perfect or one or two mistakes = 1, more than two mistakes = 0) was r = .684, even higher than the correlation with the four-value scoring system!

That this second two-value scoring system would result in a higher correlation indicates the theoretical point that what really counts in SRTs is not a verbatim, error free, repetition of the sentence, but rather repetition of the sentences with only one or two errors per sentence. If future SRTs wish to go over to a two value system, I strongly recommend the second of the above systems, where value "1" is ascribed to a perfect repetition, or one that has only one or two mistakes, and value "0" is ascribed to a repetition with three or more mistakes.

Switching to a two-value system is a viable possibility. When I re-selected fifteen sentences for the short SRT, using as criteria the difficulty level and the discrimination index based on the second two-value scoring system, the coefficient of correlation between the results on the fifteen sentences and the RPE was r = .698. This compares favorably to the coefficient of correlation between the RPE and the short SRT with the fifteen sentences chosen using the difficulty level and the discrimination index based on the four-value scoring system (r = .681).

One disadvantage of switching over to the second two-value system is that more of the sentences included on the final form of the SRT would have to be chosen from the longer, more difficult sentences used on the long form of the

SRT. This could slightly increase the time and difficulty of administering an individual test. Longer sentences would have to be used to increase the number of mistakes in repetition. Since this second two-value scoring system is very forgiving, giving a subject the full value of a correct response even if he or she had one or two errors in the repetition, perfect scores would be too easy to achieve for the more proficient speakers of Sango. This logically brings about the necessity of including harder sentences in the test to be able to distinguish among the higher levels of bilingualism, since the harder sentences would force more mistakes and thus avoid perfect scores among those having higher levels of bilingualism.

Choosing the final fifteen sentences

When Barrie Wetherill suggested looking "at the individual sentence tables of SRT score versus RPE level while the trial is proceeding", he seems to have the goal of choosing the sentences that are more "discriminating". By "discriminating", I believe he means sentences whose results can well predict the RPE level. If a particular sentence had level 4 people scoring 0 and level 1 people scoring 3 (perfect), then that particular sentence was less "discriminating". It did not predict well the RPE level from the performance on that sentence. Because of this desire to take into consideration the value of the individual sentences in predicting RPE levels, I decided to experiment by modifying Radloff's discrimination index so that it would be more effective in choosing sentences that would better predict the RPE levels.

As described in chapter 4, Radloff's discrimination index is arrived at by first ordering the subjects by their total scores on the preliminary form of the SRT. Then, the sentences are ordered according to their total scores (difficulty). The individual scores of the subjects are filled in before the next step.[7] Next, each sentence's scores are rearranged so that all of the 0s are together, all the 1s, etc. This rearrangement is put in a line next to the original scores (the original scores having been arranged by the overall scores of the subjects). For each subject, the difference between the original score on that sentence, and the rearranged score that is found on the next line is calculated. The total of these differences makes up the discrimination index.[8] A lower

---

[7]I found it easier to first enter the subjects' individual scores on a spreadsheet, then to total each individual's scores, then to sort the spreadsheet so that the subjects are ordered by their total scores, then to total the individual scores of the sentences, and then to sort the spreadsheet so that the sentences are in the order of increasing difficulty.

[8]For a comprehensive explanation of how to calculate the discrimination index, see Radloff 1991:45–48.

discrimination index indicates that a particular sentence can be more "effective in discriminating among performances of subjects displaying the varying levels of proficiency" (Radloff 1991:45).

I modified Radloff's discrimination index by ordering the subjects not by their total scores on the preliminary form of the SRT, but rather by their RPE levels. In this manner, the discrimination index becomes a "predictability index". This predictability index would best select the sentences that would predict results on the RPE, or best predict competence in the language in question.

The predictability index is arrived at by first ordering the subjects by their scores on the Reported Proficiency Exam (RPE). Then, the sentences are ordered according to their total scores (difficulty). The individual scores of the subjects are filled in before the next step. Next, each sentence's scores are rearranged so that all of the 0s are together, all the 1s, etc. This rearrangement is put in a line next to the original scores (the original scores having been arranged by the overall scores of the subjects). For each subject, the difference between the original score on that sentence, and the rearranged score that is found on the next line is calculated. The total of these differences makes up the predictability index. In other words, the predictability index is calculated just like the discrimination index, except that the subjects are ordered not by their total scores on the preliminary form of the SRT, but rather by their RPE levels. A lower score on this predictability index indicates that a particular sentence better predicts RPE levels from SRT repetition of that sentence.

When SRTs were first being developed by Radloff and the SIL South Asia Survey Team, they considered using the predictability index instead of the discrimination index. I believe they shied away from the predictability index at that time for fear of circularity of reasoning. They did not want to choose the final fifteen sentences with a measure based on the RPE because they thought that the correlation between the final form of the SRT and the RPE would become flawed by this circularity. This circularity is pertinent when the final SRT scores are extracted from the original, longer, SRT and then correlated and compared to the RPE scores. When a group is tested by the final SRT and by the RPE, and these scores are correlated and compared, no danger of circularity exists. Thus, correlations between extracted results of final SRTs and RPEs are flawed by the circularity of choosing sentences that predict the RPE results and then predicting RPE results with those sentences. However, choosing sentences that predict the RPE results is a better choice, because the goal is devising a test that best measures competence in language.

The logical conclusion, in order to avoid circularity of reasoning and to have a test that measures language competence as well as possible, is to develop the final SRT with the predictability index. Then, a group of subjects must be tested with the final SRT measure and the RPE measure (or other external proficiency measure), and only the correlations and comparisons of this test are useable. This would be more in line with accepted academic procedures than working with extracted scores since many other factors, such as test fatigue, can enter into the picture.

The basis for using the predictability index is the assumption that the sentences that best predict RPE levels for one sample group will also best predict RPE levels for other similar sample groups. In order to choose the sentences for the final form that best predict RPE levels, a measure of predictability is desirable.

When I re-chose the fifteen sentences of the Sango SRT based on the difficulty level and the predictability index (instead of the difficulty level and the discrimination index), the coefficient of correlation between the RPE and the new short SRT was $r = .783$.[9] The coefficient of correlation between the RPE and the old short SRT was $r = .681$. This difference in coefficients indicates that the new short SRT will probably correlate better with the RPE. Thus, it is found advisable to use the predictability index in the place of the discrimination index.

After re-selecting the fifteen sentences of the new short Sango SRT, I decided to refer to individual sentence tables of SRT score versus RPE level while the trial is proceeding. I desired to know if, based on these tables, there were any advisable changes in the selection of the sentences. I found two changes that I thought advisable. Each of the changes was the replacement of one sentence with another sentence having the same predictability index. When I recalculated the coefficient of correlation between the RPE and the changed fifteen sentences, the results jumped slightly to $r = .790$ ($.783$ before the two changes).

---

[9]This coefficient of correlation is only given for comparison purposes with the coefficient of correlation between the RPE and the old short SRT. As the new short SRT score is extracted from the preliminary, long SRT, this coefficient only has comparative value and cannot be said to represent the relationship between the new short SRT and the RPE. In order to represent that relationship, a new group must be tested with the new, short form of the SRT and the RPE. I will continue to present coefficients of correlation based on extracted data in this paper with the understanding that they are only for comparative purposes in the development of SRTs, and do not represent relationships between the testing measures.

Choosing the final fifteen sentences

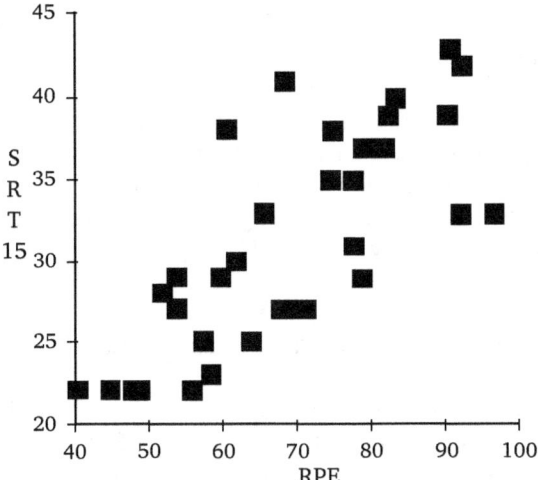

Figure 5.1 SRT-15 by RPE: Sentence chosen with predictability index and individual charts

I attribute this small jump not to the lack of value of referring to the individual sentence tables, but rather to the high value of the predictability index, which was devised to meet the same goal as the individual sentence tables. When I applied the individual sentence tables to investigate changes in sentences that were chosen with the discrimination index, I found many of the same changes that the predictability index called for. In general, I think that the predictability index and the individual sentence tables do approximately the same thing. However, I found the predictability index much easier to use. Therefore, I recommend using the predictability index, followed by reference to individual sentence tables. The individual sentence tables can reveal one sentence superior to another, both sentences having the same predictability index.

When I tried selecting sentences using the predictability index on data based on two-value scoring, the coefficient of correlation between the RPE and the short form of the SRT jumped from $r = .698$ for the fifteen sentences chosen with the discrimination index to $r = .734$ for the fifteen sentences chosen with the predictability index. The jump was not as great as the jump for the data based on four-value scoring because with only two-value scoring, the predictability index has less to work with, so is less powerful. This, in itself is an argument against using a two-value scoring system.

When I then referred to the individual sentence tables of SRT scores versus RPE levels, and re-selected the fifteen sentences for the data based on two-value scoring, the coefficient of correlation between the RPE and the newly chosen fifteen sentences was r = .765. In this case, referring to the individual sentence tables was more valuable than in the case of the four-value data due to the fact that, for the two-value data, the predictability index is not powerful. Thus, the sentences that would best predict the RPE level were not selected, so, when I referenced the sentence tables for the two-value scoring data, they revealed which sentences would be more predictive of the RPE levels.

Difficulty levels as a criterion of choice

My next step was to investigate if I could find sentences for the final form of the SRT that would be even more predictive of the RPE levels by selecting sentences that had higher difficulty levels, still referring to the predictability index and the individual sentence tables. Fifteen sentences covering a range of difficulty, but all with a difficulty level over .2, were chosen. The coefficient of correlation between the RPE and this new experimental set of SRT sentences was r = .555, considerably lower than that of the set of sentences that represented a full range of difficulty (r = .787).

After this, I investigated if I could find sentences for the final form of the SRT that would be even more predictive of the RPE levels by selecting sentences that had lower difficulty levels, still referring to the predictability index and the individual sentence tables. Fifteen sentences covering a range of difficulty, but all with a difficulty level under .25 were chosen. The coefficient of correlation between the RPE and this new experimental set of SRT sentences was r = .790, virtually the same as that of the set of sentences that represented a full range of difficulty (r = .787). As there were relatively few subjects in that sample with RPE levels of over 4, I thought it best to maintain the set of SRT sentences that represented a full range of difficulty. Although the experimental set of sentences predicted the RPE results for this sample as well as the sentences that represented a full range of difficulty, they might not do so for a sample with more subjects in the higher ranges of RPE results. In general, however, it appears that these results indicate that the less difficult sentences better predict RPE results.

SRT final form—RPE correlation

The final form of the SRT (fifteen sentences) was used to test 61 subjects, who had previously been evaluated by the RPE. This testing took place in Yalouké between March 3–12, 1993, and in Londo in the spring of 1994, both in the CAR. When plotted on a scattergram, these data showed the distribution indicated in figure 5.2.

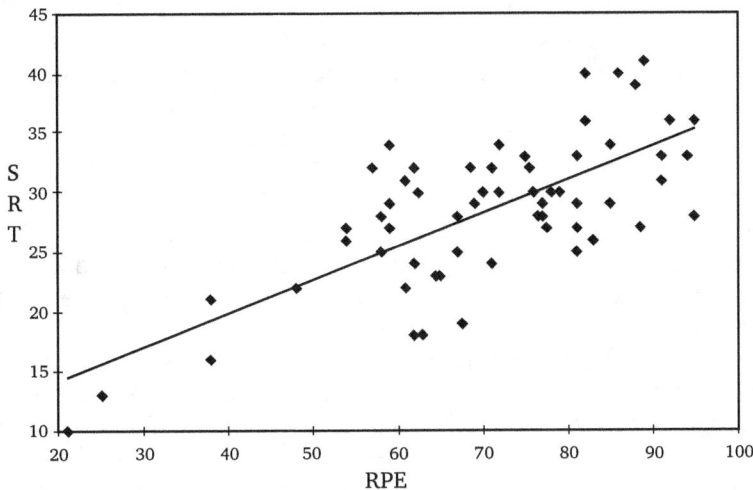

Figure 5.2: Final SRT-15 RPE correlation

This distribution indicates a significant correlation (P = .001, Multiple R = 0.71) between the SRT and the RPE for these data. It can be noted that there were very few subjects who scored less than 50 on the RPE. For this reason, the coefficient of correlation for these data (r = .71) does not reflect the tightness of the correlation. The reason why there are so few subjects in the 30–50 RPE range is that the RPE must be done with educated mother-tongue speakers, and in the CAR where one finds educated mother-tongue speakers of Sango, one has difficulty finding people who do not speak Sango well. It appears that Bossangoa was a better location than Yalouké and Londo for finding both mother tongue speakers of Sango and people who do not speak Sango well. In the future, it is planned to test more subjects with both the RPE and the SRT in order to have more subjects in the low RPE ranges.

From figure 5.2 statements could be made predicting RPE language level results from SRT results. A score of under 25 on the SRT probably indicates a RPE score of under 70 which is level 3 or below. A score of over 35 on the SRT probably indicates a RPE score of over 80 which is a very high level 3+ or above.

Conclusions concerning modifications of SRT procedures

These experiments indicate the use of the predictability index, followed by reference to individual sentence tables of SRT scores versus RPE levels, to choose the sentences for the final form of the SRT. As the predictability index appears to be so strong when used with four-value scoring data, perhaps it could be used without the reference to individual sentence tables, for those who have difficulty constructing such tables.

The use of the predictability index necessitates testing a new sample with the final form of the SRT and the RPE in order to see the resulting correlation, and to see how predictive the SRT scores are of RPE levels.

I recommend staying with the four-value scoring system, not because it better predicts RPE levels from the SRT, but because the predictability index is stronger and more useful in choosing the sentences to be included in the final form of the SRT when it is based on a four-value scoring system.

The lower coefficient-of-correlation resulting from using sentences with higher difficulty levels suggests that the best results are obtained from either a full range of difficulty of sentences or from sentences of lesser difficulty.

All of the above experiments are based on the assumption that the sentences that best predict RPE levels when extracted from the long form of the SRT are the ones that predict RPE levels for other samples. I believe this is a safe working assumption. But, I recognize that the only way to truly perform these experiments if the assumption is not accepted would be to create multiple final forms of the SRT and then correlate these against RPE results.

I recommend that future SRTs maintain the four-value scoring system, use the predictability index, if possible refer to individual sentence tables after using the predictability index, and always include a correlation of the final form of the SRT with the external proficiency index based on a fresh group of subjects.

Data gathering and coding

The data gathering for the SRT in Sango was done in collaboration with the SIL regional survey team. This team adopted the Sango SRT as their assessment tool to measure competence in Sango.

An individual subject scoring sheet was prepared for the SRT. Appendix 4 contains a copy of this individual subject scoring sheet. This sheet first has blanks for information about the subject. A survey technician questions the subject and records the information in the appropriate blanks. The information requested includes the subject's name, address, age, sex, mother tongue, household language, work language, occupation, language of education, level of education, and the mother tongue of the subject's mother, father, and spouse.

For data management purposes, each subject is given a number, which is also recorded on the scoring sheet, as well as the name of the test administrator, tape technician, and the date. For those subjects who were evaluated with the RPE, the name of the evaluator is also included on the SRT individual subject recording sheet.

After this information was recorded, the subject's residence history was recorded. The subject was asked to name the places where he or she had lived for more than one year. For each residence location, the length of residence and the actual years of residence were recorded.

The test administrator then demonstrated the use of the headphones, placing a set on themselves, while explaining to the subject that they were going to hear some sentences, and that the subject's job would be to repeat the sentences exactly as they heard them.

After an adjustment of the playback volume, the second set of headphones was placed on the subject, and the first practice sentence was played. The first practice sentence is made up of only four simple words. The administrator would then give a nonverbal signal to the subject to repeat the sentence. In most cases the subject would repeat the sentence as they heard it. In the rare cases that the subject would not repeat the sentence correctly, either not saying anything or giving a type of commentary on the sentence, the administrator would again tell the subject to simply repeat the sentence, saying something like, "You hear in the earphones, 'I'm going to the market', you should say, 'I'm going to the market.'"

The second practice sentence is then played. And in the overwhelming majority of the cases the subject would correctly repeat the sentence. In the rare cases where the subject did not repeat the second practice sentence correctly, the process was again explained and acted out for the subject, and the practice sentences were repeated. Less than once per hundred subjects, a prospective subject would still not repeat the practice sentences correctly and thus be dropped from the testing process.

After the correct, verbatim repetition of the second practice sentence, the administrator told the subject that there were more sentences to repeat, and that the sentences would get longer and more difficult, but the subject should do his/her best to repeat them exactly as they were spoken. The test sentences were played, the subjects would repeat each sentence directly after the sentence was given, and the administrator would make note of any and all aspects of the repetition which were not identical to the given sentence.

One point was subtracted for any individual difference between the test sentence and the repeated sentence, up to the maximum of 3 points per sentence. Thus, a sentence that was repeated identically to the test sentence would receive three points, a sentence repeated with only one mistake would receive two points, a sentence which was repeated with two mistakes would receive one point, and a sentence which was repeated with three or more mistakes would receive no points.

The list of possible mistakes, all causing the loss of one point are: omissions, order changes, added word or phrase, wrong word substituted, a mangled word, repetition of a word or phrase, a correction, or restart. As the test consists of fifteen sentences, and a sentence repeated correctly receives three points, the highest possible score is 45.

There were 706 subjects tested with the SRT. The individual data sheets were coded onto a Microsoft Excel spreadsheet. For each subject, the data fields listed in table 5.1 were included.

Table 5.1 Data fields included in coding

SRT results	1–45
age (in decade)	1,2,3,4,5,6,7,8,
sex	M,F
mother tongue	language name
household language	language name
work language	language name
parents language same or different from each other	S,D
spouse's language same or different from subject	S,D
occupation	agricultural, unemployed, skilled, commerce, professional, government
educational level (average years)	0,1,3,6,10,13
residence area	rural, urban, Bangui
residence history	never in urban, urban, Bangui
residence	town name
subject number	number
subject name	name

The Microsoft Excel Spreadsheet was imported into the Data Desk 4.1 (1993) data analysis program. Data pattern exploration was carried out

Data gathering and coding 59

through that program. Various data display charting options, ANOVA (analysis of variance), and regression analyses were used to discover the data patterns presented in chapters 6 and 7.

For the ANOVA analysis, the dependent variable is the SRT results. The independent variables are age, sex, parents' language (same or different from each other), spouse's language (same or different from the subject), occupation, education, residence, and residence history.

For the regression analyses, the SRT was again the dependent variable. As a regression needs numerical data, certain derived variables were created to allow inclusion of noncontinuous data in the regression. For instance, the gender variable was translated to 0 for male and 1 for female. The regression analysis would then be sensitive to how the SRT results for females differed from the results for males.

For the first regression analysis, the independent variables were continuous variables and derived variables. The continuous variables were age, years of education, geographical distance (the geographic distance between the subject's home area and Bangui), and genetic distance (the degree of linguistic relatedness between Sango and the mother tongue of the subject). The derived variables were Banguist (whether or not the subject had ever lived in Bangui), Bangui (whether or not the subject currently lived in Bangui), urbhist (whether or not the subject had ever lived in an urban region), old trade (whether or not the subject came from an area on or near the old riverian trade routes), gender, work (whether or not the subject had a higher or lower occupation), spouse same (whether or not the subject and their spouse had the same mother tongue), and parents same (whether or not the subject's parents shared the same mother tongue). These variables are further discussed in the next chapters along with the presentation of the results.

6

The Treatment of SRT Data: Social Factors

In this chapter, results of the SRT are presented. Statistical treatments of the data and observations drawn from the data are also presented, along with tentative explanations of apparent patterns.

The presentation of the data is based on different social factors that do, or do not, correlate with competence in Sango, as revealed by the SRT. First, regression and analysis of variation statistics are presented. These reveal what social factors play an important role in predicting competence in Sango. Next individual social factors and their effects are discussed.

The social factors discussed in this chapter are those which can be attributed to individuals, such as sex, age, education, occupation, residence, residence history, parents' language, and spouse's language. Factors which can be attributed to the society in whole, such as the location of the language group, or the genetic classification of the language group, are discussed in chapter 7.

Analysis of variance (ANOVA)

After the SRT data were compiled and entered into a database, the data were entered into the Data Desk 4.1 data management application. An analysis of variance (ANOVA) was applied. The ANOVA analysis tests the hypothesis that means from the samples are equal, thus indicating they are drawn from the same population. Thus, with the ANOVA analysis, a probability of 0.001 for a particular variable means that the statistical tool separated the data into different samples, which were determined by the different values of the variant, and tested the hypothesis that these samples came from the same population. This analysis found that the probability of these samples coming from the same population was one in a thousand, thus indicating that the variable in question had an effect on the results. The ANOVA analysis gave the results shown in table 6.1.

Table 6.1 ANOVA For SRT

No Selector

Source	df	Sums of Squares	Mean Square	F-ratio	Prob.
Constant	1	539934	539934	18197	≤0.0001
Age	10	853.41	185.341	6.2466	≤0.0001
Sex	1	7.36890	7.36890	0.24836	0.6184
Parents' lang.	1	65.6860	65.6860	2.2138	0.1372
Spouse's lang.	2	76.9919	38.4960	1.2974	0.2739
Occupation	6	128.376	21.3960	0.72111	0.6327
Education	7	1528.44	218.349	7.3591	≤0.0001
Residence	2	601.847	300.924	10.142	≤0.0001
Residence history	3	1198.09	399.363	13.460	≤0.0001
Error	674	19998.1	29.6708		
Total	706	43347.9			

Age, education, residence, and residence history are all revealed to be strong factors in this ANOVA treatment of the data. A similar statistic, regression analysis, revealed the same associations.

Regression analysis

Regression analysis is a statistical tool which is used to study the relationship between a dependent variable (a response variable) and independent variables (explanatory variables). Using the least squares method, it is designed to predict the behavior of the dependent variable from the values of the independent. As a regression analysis calls for data in numeric form, certain derived variables were created in the Data Desk format to enable the application of the regression analysis statistic. Such an analysis is presented in table 6.2.

Table 6.2 Regression analysis

Source	Sum of Squares	df	Mean Square	F-ratio
Regression	22527.9	12	1877.32	62.5
Residual	20819.5	693	30.0426	

Variable	Coefficient	s.e. of coeff.	t-ratio	prob
Constant	18.8101	1.107	17.0	≤0.0001
Age	−0.986755	0.1502	−6.57	≤0.0001
EducYears	0.699566	0.0836	8.37	≤0.0001
Banghist	5.09383	0.7182	7.09	≤0.0001
Bangui	3.51917	0.7019	5.01	≤0.0001
Urbhist	2.70478	0.6377	4.24	≤0.0001
OldTrade	2.16352	0.4281	5.05	≤0.0001
GeogrDistance	0.550175	0.1929	2.85	0.0045
GeneticDistance	0.179635	0.1798	0.999	0.3182
Gender	0.601339	0.4595	1.31	0.1911
Work	−0.820247	0.5573	−1.47	0.1415
SpouseSame	0.987151	0.5844	1.69	0.0916

Dependent variable is: SRT
No Selector
707 total cases of which 1 is missing
R squared = 52.0% R squared (adjusted) = 51.1%
s = 5.481 with 706 − 13 = 693 degrees of freedom

The coefficient column in table 6.2 is important in discussing the relative strength of effect of factors affecting the SRT scores. In order to determine this strength, the procedure is to multiply the absolute value of the coefficient by the range of the variable (number of possible values minus 1). Table 6.3 provides these strength of effects. Similar to the ANOVA statistic, the regression analysis with the strength of effects calculation reveals that age, education, whether or not one lives in Bangui, whether or not one lived in Bangui (Banghist), and whether or not one lived in an urban center (Urbhist), are strong factors in predicting competence in Sango. GeogrDistance, the geographical distance between the center of the Sango language and the center of the language spoken as the mother tongue of the subjects, GeneticDistance, the genetic closeness of relationship between Sango and the mother tongue of the subjects, and OldTrade, whether or not the geographical center of the language spoken as a mother tongue is on or near an old trade route, are discussed in chapter 7.

Table 6.3 Strength of effect of independent variables

Age	6.9
EducYears	8.4
Banghist	5.1
Bangui	3.5
Urbhist	2.7
OldTrade	4.3
GeogrDistance	2.2
GeneticDistance	1.1
Gender	0.6
Work	0.8
SpouseSame	1.0
ParentSame	0.8

Gender

The ANOVA and the regression statistics above show that gender does not play a large role in predicting bilingualism in Sango (strength of effect = 0.6). However, in figure 6.1, which presents SRT results for male and for female for each generation, it can be seen that there is a gender difference in the patterning of the results.

Regression analysis

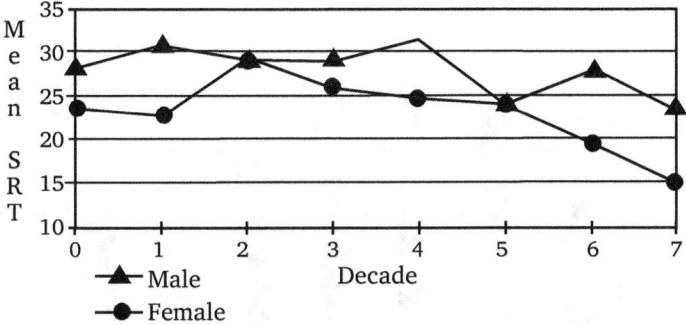

Figure 6.1 SRT by gender and age

Men and women seem to demonstrate different patterns of acquisition of Sango. Figure 6.1 reveals that the all the men under the age of forty perform similarly, while the younger women, those in their twenties and not up to their forties, are the ones who are competent in Sango. These observations corroborate observations reported on in chapter 8 which reveal that the men had more of a traditional opportunity to learn and use Sango, and that it is only recently that the women are beginning to use Sango as much.

Age

As seen from both the ANOVA and the multiple regression statistics with strength of effect, age is an important factor in predicting competence in Sango. The strength of effect of 6.9 (table 6.3) places age as one of the stronger factors. Figure 6.2 presents the average SRT results for the different age groups. The grouping of age is done by decade: 0 represents 0-9 years old, 1 represents 10–19 years old, 2 represents 20–29 years old, and so on.

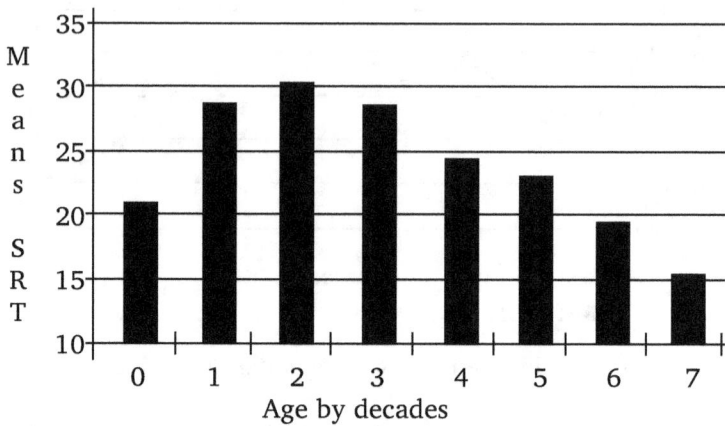

Figure 6.2 SRT by age

It can be seen from this chart that age has a large effect on Sango competency. In general, younger people had better scores on the SRT than older people. The older someone is, the more likely he or she is to perform poorly on the SRT and has less of a grasp of Sango.

Those in their twenties have the highest average score on the SRTs, even higher than those under twenty. This distribution of data reveals that Sango is a second language for most of the population of the CAR. Many people only have the opportunity to fully acquire Sango as they enter into their adult years.

This pattern of age grading also reveals that Sango is spreading at a fast rate. People between ten and forty years of age demonstrate a high level of competence in Sango, as revealed by the SRT, much higher than those over forty years of age. This fact indicates a fast rate of spread and is indicative of a change in progress of habitual speech choices.

This pattern of age grading is also seen with language internal changes (sociolinguistic variables). In time of active language internal change, the young are well advanced of the old, and the very young will not always be at the top of the change, giving the mid-high-low contour. Also, in times of active change, differences between male and female performance are common. It is noteworthy that the SRT results present similar sex and age distribution patterns.

From figure 6.1 it can be seen that the male and the female subjects have different contours of competence in Sango. It appears that all of the men, from forty years and younger, have a good grasp of Sango. The average SRT score for mother-tongue speakers of Sango living in Bangui was

34. Mother-tongue speakers of Sango living in other urban areas averaged 31 while those living in rural areas averaged 27. Figure 6.1, shows that the scores of the male subjects in their forties and under are clustered around 30. The women who are in their twenties have a correspondingly good grasp of Sango (average score 29), but those younger than twenty and older than thirty have less of a grasp of Sango. This would seem to reveal different patterns of acquisition of Sango for men and for women. The men are in the forefront of the acquisition, and the young women of this generation are now catching up.

The age pattern seen in figure 6.2 is largely due to the behavior of women. As can be seen from figure 6.1 where the results of the women and men are presented separately, it is the women who peak in the twenties. This pattern is not seen in the men's results, but can be seen in the combined chart of age grading, figure 6.2, because of the strength of the women's age grading contour. All the men under fifty have averaging scores equally high in Sango. The women under fifty show more age grading, with those in their twenties showing the highest abilities in Sango.

Occupation

In the ANOVA analysis and also in the regression analysis, the factor of occupation did not play a large role in predicting competence in Sango (0.8 strength of effect from table 6.3). However, charting the average SRT results for the different occupations gives the chart in figure 6.3.

From this chart, it is evident that those whom we would expect to control Sango better do, in fact, score higher on the SRT. The subjects who were students or government workers had an average SRT of 32 while those involved in agriculture had an average SRT of only 24 (average score for mother-tongue speakers of Sango is 33). The other professions are ranked between these two extremes, giving an ordering of professions that could well represent a scale of how important language is for these different professions in the linguistic market.

This distribution of the data would make it appear that occupation is an important correlating factor of the spread of a language. A person's need to communicate in the linguistic market seems to reflect itself in how well and how soon that individual learns the spreading language. However, the ANOVA analysis and the low strength of effect from the regression analysis (0.8) provide evidence that occupation is not a strong factor in predicting competence in Sango.

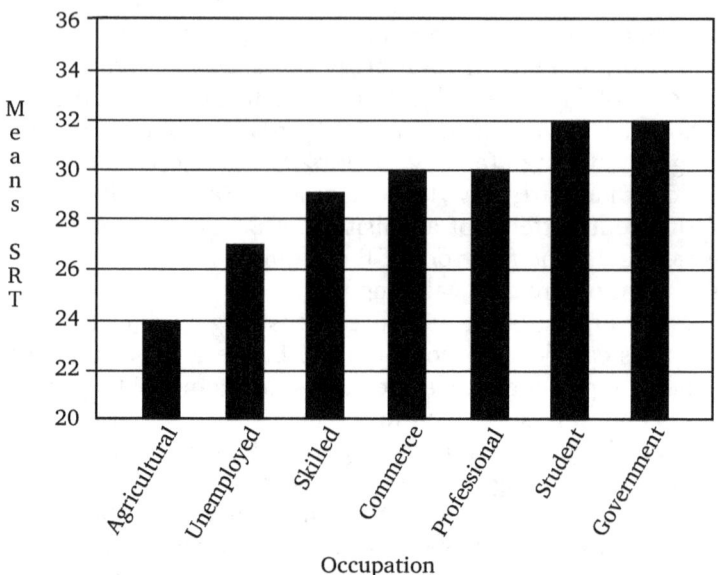

Figure 6.3 SRT by occupation

The question then arises as to why the factor of occupation did not reveal itself to be a strong factor in predicting competence in Sango on either the ANOVA analysis or the regression analysis. The factor of occupation correlates with other factors such as education and residence or previous residence in Bangui or in urban areas. For instance, students and government workers are among the best educated, and most of these have been in Bangui for their studies. Concerning the residence factors, farmers are not found in cities, and professionals are usually not found in rural areas. The factors of education and the residence factors better explain the overall variation than does occupation. Thus, even though there is a correlation between SRT results and occupation, occupation is not revealed as a strong factor in predicting competence in Sango. ANOVA and regression analyses without the factors of education, and without the geographical residence factors reveal that occupation is a strong predictor. In an ANOVA analysis where the education and residence factors were dropped, occupation had an F-ration of 18.3 and a probability of ≤ 0.0001. In a similar regression analysis, where the residence and education factors were excluded, the strength of effect for the occupation factor was 4.8.

This distribution of SRT results by occupation indicates a pattern where the higher social-economic classes have higher scores on not only prestige sociolinguistic variants, but also on prestige varieties in language shift situations.

Residence

The ANOVA and the regression analyses reveal that subjects' place of actual residence is a strong factor in predicting SRT results. Those who were living in Bangui scored higher than those who were not. Those who were living in other urban centers scored higher than those who were in more rural areas. Figure 6.4 presents a graphic image of this quantitative demonstration of the rural/urban axes. The means SRT for those living in Bangui is over 33 which is the same average as those claiming Sango as their mother tongue. The means SRT for those living in other urban areas is 28, and the means SRT for those living in rural areas is 24. Thus, we see here the process of the language of wider communication, Sango, spreading out from the main urban area, Bangui, to the other urban areas, and then to the rural areas. This pattern of the spread of an innovation from major urban to minor urban to rural areas is identical to the pattern of the spread of innovations within one language.

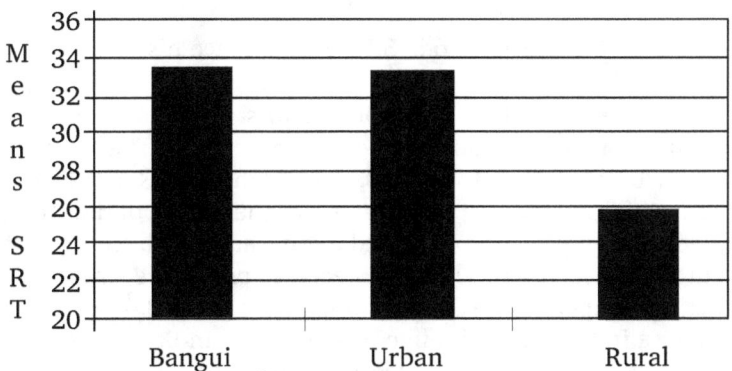

Figure 6.4 SRT by residence

Residence history

The factor of the subjects' residence history also proved to be a strong factor in predicting competence in Sango and thus performance on the SRT. Those who had at some time in their life lived in Bangui performed better than those who had not. Those who had at some time in their life lived in some other urban area performed better than those who had not. The chart in figure 6.5 presents this factorial relationship and again graphically displays a quantitative demonstration of the rural/urban axes. This factor and chart differs from the Residence chart in firgure 6.4 which refers to actual residence at the time of testing, and the chart in figure 6.5 refers to a history of residence, whether or not the subjects had ever lived in either Bangui or some other urban center.

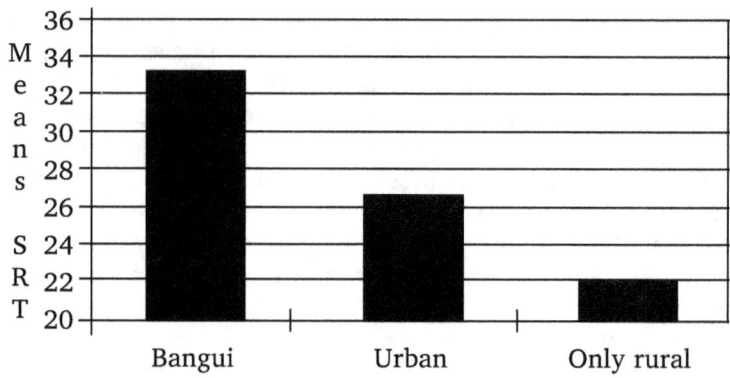

Figure 6.5 SRT by residence history

These residence factors are strong factors. From table 6.3, we see that the strength of effect of those living in Bangui is 3.5. The strength of effect of those who have ever lived in Bangui (Banguist) is 5.1. Because of the similarity of these factors, and because of the nature of the strength of effect, these two figures can be added to give an overall strength of effect of Bangui residence of 8.6. This then becomes one of the strongest factors in predicting competence in Sango, comparable to the 8.4 for years of education. Those individuals who live or have lived in Bangui, where Sango is the language of choice, show higher degrees of competence in Sango.

Individuals who had lived in Bangui or, to lesser degrees, in other urban areas performed much better on the SRT. This again demonstrates that the distribution of relative bilingualism in a spreading language is mostly based on factors associated with individuals.

Parents' language

Whether or not a subject's parents shared the same mother tongue is another factor which does not show up in the ANOVA and the regression as very strong, but it does show a strong pattern of distribution. This is most probably due to the fact that most mixed marriages are in the urban areas. The residence factors and the parents' language factor correlate: 22 percent of subjects living in Bangui reported that their parents had different mother tongues. Outside of Bangui, only 7 percent of the subjects reported that their parents had different mother tongues. As the factors which refer to residence better explain the variation than the parents' language factor, the parents' language factor is not revealed as a strong factor on the statistical analyses.

An ANOVA analysis, which excluded the residence and education factors, assigned an F-ration of 7.7 and a probability of 0.0001 to the parents' language factor. A similar regression analysis attributed a moderate strength of effect ($= 2.1$).

Figure 6.6 shows the average SRT results for subjects with parents sharing and not sharing a mother tongue. As Sango is the language of choice for communication between ethnic groups, this is exactly what would be expected. Households where the mother and father spoke different languages would most likely be households where Sango was spoken. Thus, those who come from these households would know Sango much better.

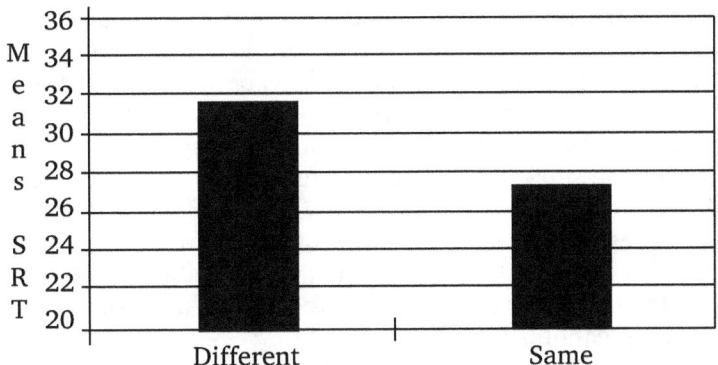

Figure 6.6 SRT by parents' language

Spouse's language

Whether or not a subject spoke the same mother tongue as his or her spouse was also one of the factors coded. If a subject spoke a different mother tongue than his or her spouse, the value "different" was attributed. If a subject was not married, or if his or her spouse shared a mother tongue, the value "same" was attributed. Figure 6.7 displays the average

SRT scores for those with the same or different mother tongue as their spouse.

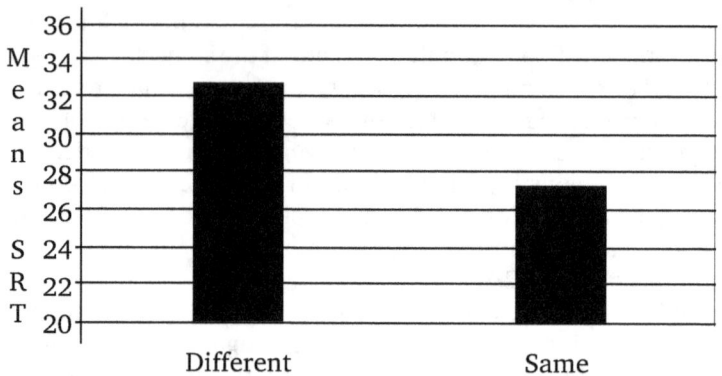

Figure 6.7 SRT by spouse's language

As expected, those who do not have the same mother tongue as their spouse are more proficient in Sango, as shown by a higher mean SRT for the group. As in the above case, this factor did not reveal itself as a strong factor in the ANOVA or regression analysis because mixed marriages are often found in urban, not rural areas. Of the subjects who lived in Bangui 34 percent claimed that they had a spouse who spoke a different mother tongue. For the subjects who never lived in Bangui this percentage was only 7 percent.

ANOVA results, when the factors of education and residence were dropped, gave an F-ration of 13.4 with a probability of 0.0001 to the spouse's language factor. A similar regression analysis gave the high strength of effect of 5.5.

Education

Education is one of the strongest factors in predicting competency in Sango, and results on the SRT bear this out. Both the ANOVA and the regression analyses show the strength of the factor. Figure 6.8 displays average SRT scores for subjects grouped according to years of education.

Regression analysis 73

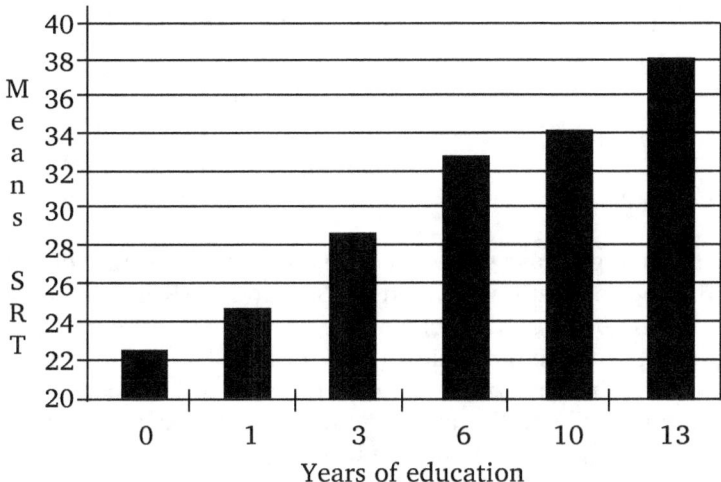

Figure 6.8 SRT by education

This distribution reveals a strong correlation between years of education and results of the SRT. From the results of the regression analysis and strength of effect calculation (strength of effect = 8.4) given above (tables 6.2 and 6.3), it can be safely stated that education is an extremely strong factor in predicting SRT results. The chart in figure 6.8, corroborated by information presented in chapter 8, shows that the longer a subject studied in school, the better that subject speaks Sango, even though the schooling is in French, not in Sango! There is a strong correlation between years of schooling, allegedly in French, and bilingualism in Sango.

At this point the question might well be raised about the possibility that the higher scores on the SRT for those who have attended school is a result of their increased test-taking skills, gained over the course of their education, and not a reflection of higher degrees of competence in Sango. To answer this question, one could refer to the correlation between the SRT and the Reported Proficiency Exam (RPE) described in chapter 5. There could be other factors, such as living along an old trade route which would not affect test taking skills, and would correlate with high results on the SRT. Speakers of Sango, living in Bangui, with and without formal educations were compared. Bangui speakers who had not been to school had a mean SRT score of 29.1, while those who had been to school for an average of 3 years had a mean score of 32.7.

Table 6.4 Mean SRT by education and Bangui residence

	Years of schooling					
	0	1	3	6	10	13
Bangui	29.1	30.1	32.7	34.3	35.9	39
N/Bangui	21.7	23.4	27.2	31.5	31.8	36

Education might have some effect on SRT results because of test-taking skills. But the correlation between the SRT and the RPE, and the distribution of results of factors which cannot be influenced by individual test-taking skills, indicate the basic validity of the SRT. The simple verbatim repetition required as a test-taking skill for the SRT is part of the traditional culture of the preliterate societies in the area where messages were to be carried without any change in wording. As Sango is used extensively at schools, it is possible that even for those living in Bangui, higher degrees of education bring about greater competence in Sango.

Some of the more educated people had more trouble with the test than the uneducated. Certain educated subjects thought that the test was too simple, that there had to be some kind of catch, that perhaps the test administrators were looking for a paraphrase or an interpretation or a commentary instead of a simple repetition. With these people, when this tendency was noticed on the sample phrases that were administered before the actual test, encouragement was given to simply repeat the sentences.

This aside, there remains the question of why schooling, allegedly in French, correlates very highly with SRT results. This question is addressed in chapter 8, where participant observation information is presented to address the question. A summary of the conclusions about this question is that (1) the social situation in the school often calls for the use of Sango; (2) Sango is, in a sub-rosa way, used in formal education; and (3) teachers seem to desire to encourage the use of Sango. Years of education correlates highly with SRT results in Sango because students learn and use Sango at the schools, both inside and outside the classroom.

This chapter has shown that there are strong similarities between the patterns of distribution of social factors concerning bilingualism and patterns of distribution of social factors concerning innovation in language change. Age, the urban/rural axis, sex, education, and social class all show similar patterns. This lends support toward the viewpoint that language shift and language change are indeed aspects of the same phenomenon.

7

The Treatment of SRT Data: The Effect of Language Differences on Bilingualism

The use in this work of the SRT allowed for a quantitative investigation into factors which correlate with bilingualism in the spreading language. The correlations found are examined to see what can be learned about the mechanisms of language shift.

The first large category of correlations and possible correlations has to do with social factors that are associated with individuals: factors such as age, education, and residence history. This was presented and discussed in chapter 6.

The second category of correlations and possible correlations with bilingualism in Sango has to do with social factors that are associated with language groups: factors such as genetic differences between the languages in the study or geographical distance from the center of the spreading language.

The investigation of possible correlations between bilingualism in the spreading language and the degree of genetic similarity between the languages in the study addresses the issue of interference in the acquisition of a spreading language. Is learning the spreading language facilitated where there are great similarities between the spreading language and the original language of a person or a group? And, do large differences between the two languages seriously inhibit the acquisition of the spreading language?

If there are correlations between bilingualism in the spreading language and similarity of L1 and L2, this implies that there are correlations between lack of, or lesser degrees of, bilingualism and differences between L1 and L2. In this case, an attempt should be made to discover what aspects of the differences between L1 and L2 prove crucial in interfering with the acquisition of the spreading language.

Correlations between distance from the geographical center of the spreading language and the centers of the language that are used as mother tongues would also reveal information about the dynamics of language spread.

Genetic differences and bilingualism

In this aspect of the data treatment, the first step was to determine if there was any relevant correlation through statistical means. The second step, which was used only if correlation was present, would be to analyze the individual test results, looking for patterns in wrong answers, in order to determine what aspects of language were involved in this type of interference.

It would be necessary to classify the mistakes in the repetition of the sentences as phonological differences, lexical/semantic differences, or morphosyntactic differences (or even morphological differences and syntactic differences). Then a data treatment would be necessary to see which of these types of differences was more common for the group or groups showing less bilingualism due to linguistic differences between the mother tongue and the spreading language.

The first step involves determining if a correlation exists between linguistic difference between the two languages and lack of bilingualism. The data was loaded into the Data Desk 4.1 data management program and two different statistical procedures were employed. The first of these was a multiple regression, using a step-up procedure, to determine if the degree of linguistic relatedness would correlate with the results of the SRT. To do this, an index of linguistic relatedness was created. The tree outline in figure 7.1 displays the classifying data from Greenberg (1966) and Monino (1988).

Genetic differences and bilingualism 77

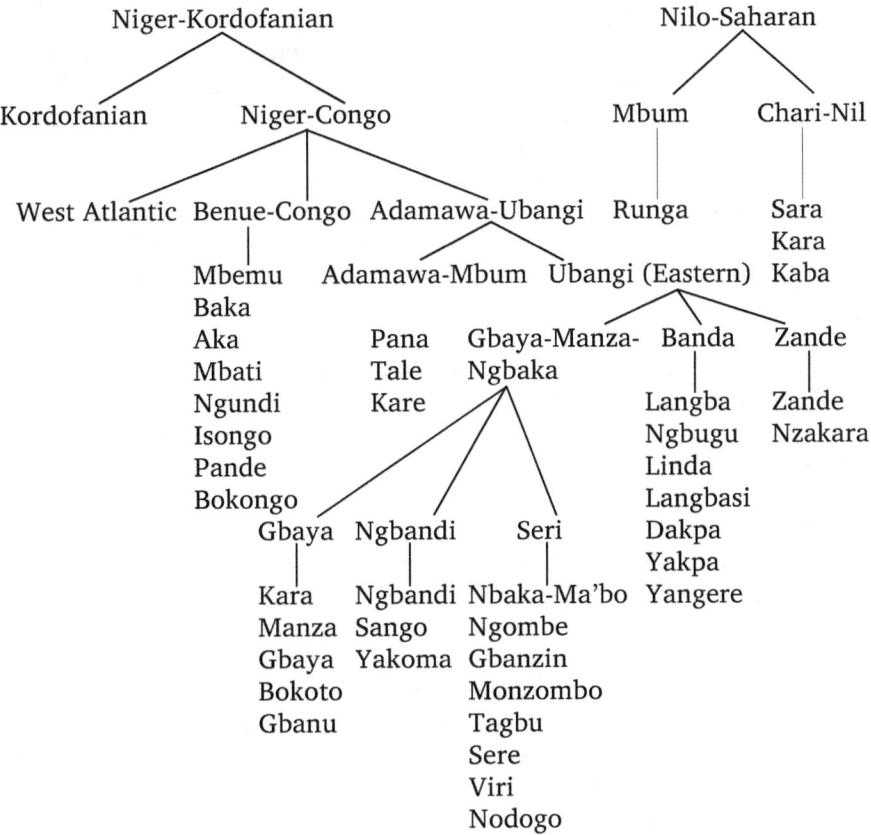

Figure 7.1 Genetic tree of CAR languages

A somewhat rough measure of linguistic relatedness was designed, providing a real number which augments as the linguistic difference between the spreading language and the mother tongue increases. The measure was created in the following way: Using the above tree diagram and starting with the node dominating Sango, count how many nodes one has to move up on the tree diagram until one is at a node that dominates the other language. The number of nodes one has to move up is the factor of linguistic relatedness.

For example, the factor of linguistic relatedness between Sango and Gbaya would be 1. Starting at the Ngbandi node, the node dominating Sango, one would have to move up one level to the Gbaya-Manza-Ngbaka node. For the degree of linguistic relationship between Sango and Aka, one would start at the Ngbandi node, move up to the Gbaya-Manza-Ngbaka node, then the Ubangi node, then the Adamawa-Ubangi node, then finally the Niger-Congo node, moving up four steps until one was at a node that dominated both Sango and Aka. Thus, the factor of linguistic relatedness between Sango and Aka would be 4.

At this point, it is important to note that there were major differences between different ethnic/language groups in how they performed on the SRT. Some groups did much better than others. The task then became one of distinguishing how much of this difference in performance between groups was due to the degree of linguistic difference between Sango and the different languages.

The regression results showed that the factor of linguistic relatedness had no significant effect on predicting SRT results. The Data Desk regression results that include the factor of linguistic relatedness (genetic distance) are displayed in table 6.2. From table 6.3 strength of effect of independent variables, it can be seen that the factor of genetic distance was not a relevant factor. It has a low strength of effect (1.1).

The strength of effect of only 1.1 (table 6.3) for genetic distance indicates that the genetic distance between Sango and the mother tongue has little if anything to do with the ability to speak Sango. This reveals that the reason the groups perform differently does not have to do with the degree of difference between their language and Sango and, therefore, there must be some other explanation. This explanation is to be found, at least partially, in the factor discussed below dealing with whether or not the center of the mother tongue of the subjects was situated on or near an old trade route.

The second statistical procedure that was employed to see if the linguistic relatedness between Sango and the mother tongue had something to do with predicting bilingualism in Sango was a cluster analysis. In this procedure factors are clustered together based on similarities that they might share. The cluster analysis was set up so that the mother tongues would be grouped together in clusters according to the similarities in their performance on the SRT. These clusters were then compared with the factors of linguistic relatedness to see if the clusters that were formed by similar performance on the SRT also revealed any patterns of grouped factors of linguistic relatedness.

The cluster analysis gave the results shown at the right of table 7.1. The left column of table 7.1 is the factor of linguistic relatedness (genetic distance). The center column is the factor of geographical distance between Bangui and the center of different languages (geographical distance).

Table 7.1 Linguistic relatedness cluster analysis

Genetic distance	Geographical distance	Language
2	3	Dagba
6	4	Vale
1	3	Gbaya of Bozoum
6	4	Kaba
6	4	Suma
1	2	Bogoto
1	3	Gbaya
1	2	Gbanu
1	3	Manza
2	4	Ngbugu
0	0	Sango
6	4	Sara
2	4	Banda

Table 7.1 reveals that there is no patterning of degree of relatedness with performance on the SRT. This again shows that the degree of linguistic relatedness between Sango and the mother tongues is not a relevant factor in predicting the results of the SRT, and thus bilingualism.

Figure 7.2 is a scatter plot that charts the means (average) of the SRTs for the language groups in each genetic distance category.

It also indicates the lack of relationship between bilingualism in Sango and the genetic similarity between Sango and mother tongue of the subjects.

These two types of tests both indicate that the linguistic distance between Sango and the mother tongue does not act as a predictor in the spread of Sango. This brings me to the conclusion that it would not be fruitful to do an extensive error analysis to determine what parts of the linguistic distance are involved, whether syntactic, morphological, phonological, or lexical/semantic. Since the statistical effect is not there, it is not reasonable to search for the cause of the nonexistent effect. In this study, the linguistic, genetic distance between the languages is not a relevant factor.

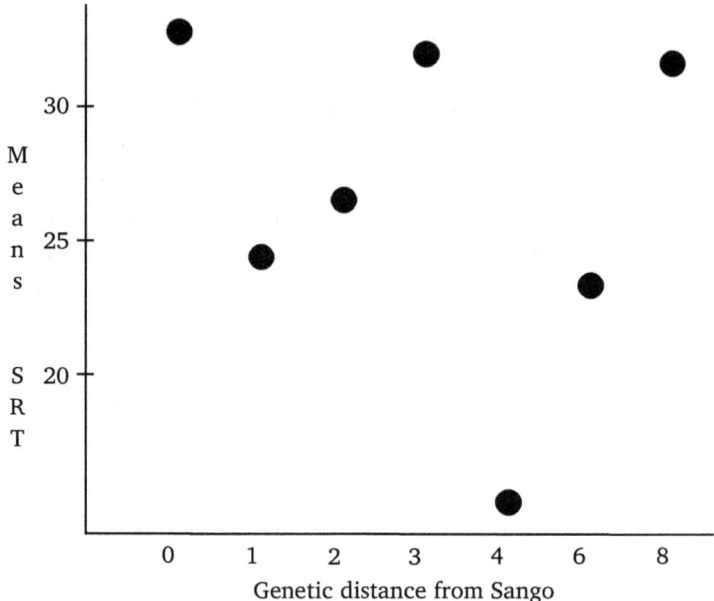

Figure 7.2 SRT by genetic relatedness of languages

Geographic distance and bilingualism

The creation of the factor of genetic distance prompted the similar creation and comparison of another factor, that of geographic distance. The factor of geographic distance was designed to assign a discrete value to the relative distance separating the center of the Sango language from the center of the other languages. This was done by measurements on a map, with those languages whose center was mapped within 1 cm. of Bangui's mapped center receiving a geographic distance factor of 1, those languages whose center was within 2 cm. of Bangui receiving a geographic distance factor of 2, and so on.

The geographical distance factors were included on the chart for the cluster analysis, along with the factors of linguistic relatedness (genetic distance). In the same manner that the chart shows no groupings of genetically related languages formed by the cluster analysis, it also shows no groupings of languages based on geographical distance.

This lack of patterning is somewhat unexpected. In the common viewpoint of diffusion of a language shift, the growing language spreads out from a particular location, covering more and more territory. This would result in a patterning of the data where there would be a grouping of languages geographically close to the center of the spreading language which would exhibit higher bilingualism, and a complementary grouping of languages that were more distant and less bilingual.

The same pattern would be expected in a regression study, where the languages that were more geographically distant would be correlated with lower degrees of bilingualism in the spreading language. The regression study that was done revealed that this patterning was present, but was only a moderate factor. The strength of effect for geographical distance was only 2.2 (table 6.3).

Surprisingly, geographical distance between the center of the Sango language and the center of the mother tongue was not a strong factor in predicting group levels of bilingualism. This can be explained by Trudgill's (1974) distinction between geographical distance and effective distance. Effective distance takes into consideration the travel routes used and the time and effort needed to travel between points. The concept of effective distance is applicable in the study of the spread of Sango, because of the history of communication and transportation in the CAR.

The history of the spread of Sango reveals that Sango spread out along the river trade routes. In the CAR area, travel by river was the main means of transportation, from long ago until fairly recently, when roads started to be built. Even today, when desiring to travel to the center of the country from Bangui, river transportation is a viable option. In chapter 8, maps made from the CAR census indicate that density of population claiming to speak Sango is higher along the traditional riverine trade routes.

Thus, a statistical analysis, using a created on or off traditional trade route factor was included in the research. This factor was created in the following way: the mother tongue/ethnic groups were divided into three categories, those on the traditional riverine trade routes, those near the traditional riverine trade routes, and those far removed from the traditional riverine trade routes.

The results of this regression analysis are shown in table 6.3. The factor OldTrade, designating whether a language group is situated on, near, or away from the old trade routes, proved to be a very strong factor. The strength of effect of the factor is 4.3. The t-ratio for the factor is 4.79, giving a probability of ≤ 0.0001. This regression analysis shows that geographical distance from the traditional riverine trade routes is a relevant factor in predicting bilingualism in Sango among these different groups.

In this chapter, social factors that are associated with larger groups were studied. Some of these factors do have a considerable affect on bilingualism in Sango. Genetic relationships between Sango and the mother tongues was not one of these factors. There was no relationship between the degree of linguistic distance and bilingualism. This was seen in both the regression statistic and the cluster analysis operation.

Geographical distance between the center of Sango and the mother-tongue areas proved to be a relevant factor in predicting bilingualism in Sango, but only a moderate factor, not a strong one.

A strong factor proved to be that of location along the ancient, riverine, trade routes. People in groups which were along the traditional trade routes were much more likely to be fluent in Sango, as demonstrated by the SRT results. People in groups that were near the old trade routes were more likely to know Sango than those where were far removed from the old trade routes. This factor (strength of effect 4.3) was much stronger than the geographical distance factor (strength of effect 2.2), demonstrating the path of language spread. Language spreads along established trade and communication routes.

The community-based factors that proved significant in predicting Sango bilingualism are factors which make reference to financial and communicative aspects of the community.

8

Participant Observation and Census Data

During my four year stay in the Central African Republic, I learned Sango to the degree that I was able to understand most if not all of what was happening around me, and was able to communicate in the appropriate manner what I desired to communicate. I was living in Bangui, the capitol, and making numerous trips to other parts of the country. My activities in Bangui included teaching sociolinguistics at the university, interfacing with many different groups and government departments, and research.

In Bangui there is an expatriate community made up of two major groups, each having a different language choice pattern. One group is the mid-east origin business community. This group often spoke Arabic among themselves and Sango with the Central Africans. The other group is made up of Europeans and American development, embassy, and religious mission workers. This group often spoke French when speaking among themselves, as well as when relating to Central Africans. As a major exception to this, many of the missionaries speak Sango with Central Africans and English among themselves. As there are visual cultural clues to indicate if any person was mid-east origin, European/American, or Central African, initial language of address is chosen using these clues.

When people knew of my connections with the religious community, they would often address me in Sango. When I was taken simply as a European or American, the first language of choice was often French. Also in this situation, Central Africans would often wrongly assume that I did not understand Sango.

Greetings are an important part of the cultural interaction in the CAR. They also serve the purpose of defining the language which will be used for the duration of the conversation. A conversation started with a greeting in French, with the greeting responded to in Sango would select Sango for the remainder of the conversation, and vice versa.

A non-mideastern origin expatriate speaking Sango was usually well received by individuals and groups. If a European or American chose to use Sango against the normal expectations, it seemed to be a type of statement of affiliation with the country, as opposed to an affiliation with the agenda or politics of France or the European Economic Community. As Sango is more associated with solidarity than is French, such a choice of Sango would often diminish officiousness and formality. This being the case, Sango quickly became my language of choice in the Central African Republic.

As the general community in the CAR includes these different expatriate groups, and as Sango is a language of wider communication and inter-group contact, in my role as an expatriate associated with teaching, development, and church activities, I was indeed a member of the larger community. Part of the data in this chapter come from my day-to-day observations as a member of this larger community. Part of the data come from informal interviews.

Participant observation—gender

When interviewing different subjects and asking the question of who speaks Sango the most, the response would often be that, in the past the men spoke Sango more, but now the women were catching up and speaking Sango a lot.

I interviewed a Peace Corps director who, twelve years before the interview, had spent two years in a small village as a Peace Corps volunteer. She said that when she was in the village she could speak Sango, but could not communicate with the women in the village because they did not speak Sango. She related an interesting experience of going back to the village in 1993, twelve years after having left the village, and was astonished that the women in the village now spoke Sango.

Two major factors have contributed to this past gender differentiation in the use of Sango. The first of these is schooling. In the past, more boys than girls attended school, and today, there are more men than women enrolled in the university. As I travel to the different areas, I regularly still see more boys than girls in the elementary schools. Because of this pattern, believed to be even more prevalent in the past, boys had more inter-group contact and more opportunity to learn and use Sango. The second main factor is that men were more likely to travel than women, particularly search of work. Again, this limited the inter-group contact that the women had. Education is becoming more and more universal for all children in the CAR, and women are traveling more than in the past.

For these reasons, I believe that women are moving from being behind in the shift toward Sango to a position where they will be leading the shift. Because control of Sango is a social asset, and because factors that limited women's contact with Sango have been changed, I, and the SRT statistics, see women moving to the traditional place of leading the change toward Sango.

The tradition of bride prices, i.e., money and goods given by the groom to the family of the bride, is an active part of many CAR cultures. I did a short interview type study of different factors that influence bride prices. How much money a groom has to pay is determined by the perceived value of the bride. This, conveniently, gives a window on the socially attributed value of different attributes of women. Certain physical characteristics of the bride can affect the amount of money the groom has to pay. Beauty, height, and ability to bear children are all positive factors that up the price. Skills, education, and money-making positions or potential held by the bride can also affect the bride price. My study revealed that a bride who speaks Sango is worth more than a bride who does not speak Sango.

Participant observation—schools

There are a number of observations I made that lead me to believe that Sango is used in the primary and secondary schools more than the official policy stipulates. Once, when in a small village, I walked toward a school, and when the teacher saw me, he switched from Sango to French. As the door which I was approaching was in the back of the classroom, I had the opportunity to observe the students before they realized I was present. When the teacher started to speak in French, there was a stir of surprise in the classroom. A number of students had a look of confusion on their faces, seemingly trying to understand what the teacher was saying. Some of the students, realizing that there must be some reason to trigger this change into French, started looking around and observed my presence.

In a large town, where I was doing some work in and around a high school, I often heard classes being conducted in Sango.

At the University of Bangui, the only university in the country, Sango is the language of choice outside of the classroom. Very often, even the expatriates who teach there learn and use Sango. Inside of the classroom, French is the language of choice. The surprisingly low level of French of some university students is another clue that Sango is widely used in elementary and secondary schools. Some university students experience trouble in understanding and communicating in French.

At one high school, after hearing Sango used in the classrooms, I was talking to one of the teachers. I mentioned that I heard a lot of Sango in the classrooms. He showed signs of discomfort and said in an explanatory manner (in French), "Sango is the national language of the country. It is necessary for the students to speak Sango."

In general, those in the education system realize the importance of French for sectors of the population in the CAR, e.g., sectors involved in international activities, or academics, or technical activities. At the same time, they see the greater importance of Sango as a national language, a language of unity and a symbol of national identity. When many of these teachers were faced with a "French only in the classroom" situation, they felt that there was a necessity to bend the rules to allow for the learning of both Sango and French.

It is also possible that a feeling of resentment against what can be interpreted as neo-colonial intervention could cause teachers to use Sango more in the classrooms. French is associated with France. Sango is associated with the CAR. If teachers had the impression that France was trying to exert undue influence on the internal workings of the government and country of CAR, such feelings would motivate teachers to to use less French and more Sango.

Furthermore, it may be that Sango is used in some classrooms for pragmatic reasons. As mentioned below, Sango is often taught to very young children by their primary care givers. These people teach Sango to the children so that the children will be advantaged in the future. Elementary school teachers find their tasks simplified in using a language that is already known by a large proportion of their students, instead of a language, French, which is often totally unknown.

Another factor to consider concerning the use of Sango in the classroom is that in all likelihood some teachers control Sango much better than they control French. In a classroom situation, this differentiation in how well these teachers control French and Sango could well encourage the use of Sango. When one has less than complete control of French in a French educational setting, speaking French can be a stressful experience. There is always the fear of making a mistake and being corrected with social stigmatization. Thus, it is possible that because of the stigmatization of mistakes that is a part of the French educational tradition, Sango becomes a more comfortable language to use in the CAR.

Participant observation—attitudes toward languages

Sango is often associated with the national identity of the Central African Republic as well as that which is modern, good, and personally advantageous in the CAR.

Once, in the city of Bossangua, in the West of CAR, I asked a young father which languages he uses at home with his family. He replied that he speaks Gbaya to his wife and Sango to his children. When I asked him why he speaks Sango to his children, he replied that Sango was the language of the future, that it was the national language, and that he wanted his children to be advantaged and be well prepared for the future.

I found this attitude among parents throughout the country. They naturally want the best for their children, and believe that their children will have a higher possibility of getting good jobs, earning money, and earning respect and status, if the children speak Sango well. Thus, to facilitate their children learning Sango, parents speak Sango to them from a very young age.

I also noticed that a good number of parents want their children to also speak the traditional ethnic language. This occurred naturally in rural areas, where the children were often learning Sango and the traditional mother tongue simultaneously. In Bangui, where children might grow up not knowing the traditional ethnic language, sending children to live with older monolingual relatives for a summer was a common activity, thus enabling the children to control the language of their immediate ancestors. Acquisition of the traditional ethnic language in this case, however, usually took second place to the felt importance of controlling Sango.

The use of French origin words, when speaking Sango is stigmatized, especially in Bangui and among the elite. In the past, use of French origin words was respected, showing that the speaker was advanced, controlling the then prestigious French. This change in attitude is spreading out from the capitol to the rural areas. Because of this, speaking with many French origin words is now associated with rural, older people who are putting on a pretension of elitism. When I was learning Sango, there was one area in which people seemed more willing to offer corrections, i.e., when I would insert a French word in a conversation, out of ignorance of the Sango word. The correction would be the offering of the appropriate Sango word.

This is surprising because, in the past for many years, Sango was liberally salted with French, both as a prestige gambit, and as a communication facilitation for those who were using Sango as a trade language. I heard leading government officials criticized because they could not give a speech in Sango without contaminating it with French words.

I observed university students engaged in a word game. They were speaking Sango, and the first one to use a French origin word would lose. One such game that I was listening to continued for thirty-two minutes before one of the contestants lost by using a French origin word.

An expatriate, when traveling to a small, remote village was complimented on her Sango ability by a pastor of a little church who had been using Sango all his life. He stated that his Sango was inferior to the Sango of this expatriate because his was not pure like that of the expatriate because he had the habit of integrating French origin words, and the expatriate did not.

The choice of using Sango often sends a social signal. That signal is one of inclusion, solidarity, and a desire for unity with those who are of other ethnic groups. Among speakers of an ethnic language, its use sends the signal of solidarity, fraternity, and a plea for special consideration. The use of French can be construed as a power gambit—a demonstration of membership in an elite class. A switch from Sango to French declares distance between the participants in the conversation.

I have observed many interactions at government offices or at airports or shipping agencies where a person seeking service would start out in French, presumably to demonstrate his or her importance and social standing, then switch to Sango as a sign of solidarity and acceptance, and as a plea for good service or even special treatment. If the one seeking service had some clue that he or she shared an ethnic identity with the person offering the service, there would be a further shift to the ethnic language. This would be a further sign of unity and solidarity and would be a strong request for good service and preferential treatment.

It is possible that this shift dynamic, teamed together with the fact that inclusion and solidarity are in themselves valued in the cultures of the CAR, is a factor in the spread of Sango. Sango, being associated with inclusion and solidarity, which in themselves are seen as positive social values, would be given impetus to be used more and more widely.

Census data—distribution of Sango speakers

In 1988, the government of the CAR sponsored and carried out a census of the population. One of the questions that was asked of each person in the country was whether or not they spoke Sango. Because the question was asked by government officials, and because speaking Sango is often seen as indicative of being a good citizen, and because in the carrying out of the survey the questions were directed to the heads of households who provided information for all of the people in their houses, it is possible that there was some over reporting in connection with this question. For someone to declare that they did not speak Sango was, in a way, declaring that the person was not a good citizen. Also, as speaking Sango is prestigious, stating that someone did not speak Sango could be seen as a challenge to the personal worth of that individual.

The census department of the CAR government (Sécretaire d'Etat au Plan aux Statistiques et à la Coopération Internationale, Bureau Central de Recensement) graciously made the census data available to the Summer Institute of Linguistics (SIL) in electronic form. At the Nairobi center of SIL, the SIL mapping project produced the data for the following map, showing the percentage of the population in each area who claim to speak Sango.

Figure 8.1 presents the average percentage of people in each area who claim to speak Sango. The numbers on the map refer to percentages of the population claiming to speak Sango. As can be seen, the great majority of people in most areas of the country claim to speak Sango. Areas with lower claimed percentages of bilingualism in Sango are found in the eastern parts of the country, the northern parts, and the western edge. There are vast uninhabited areas in the east of the country.

It is interesting to note that the areas which claim the highest percentage of competence in Sango are the areas which were most in focus in colonistic development efforts. These are areas which were accessible by available transportation.

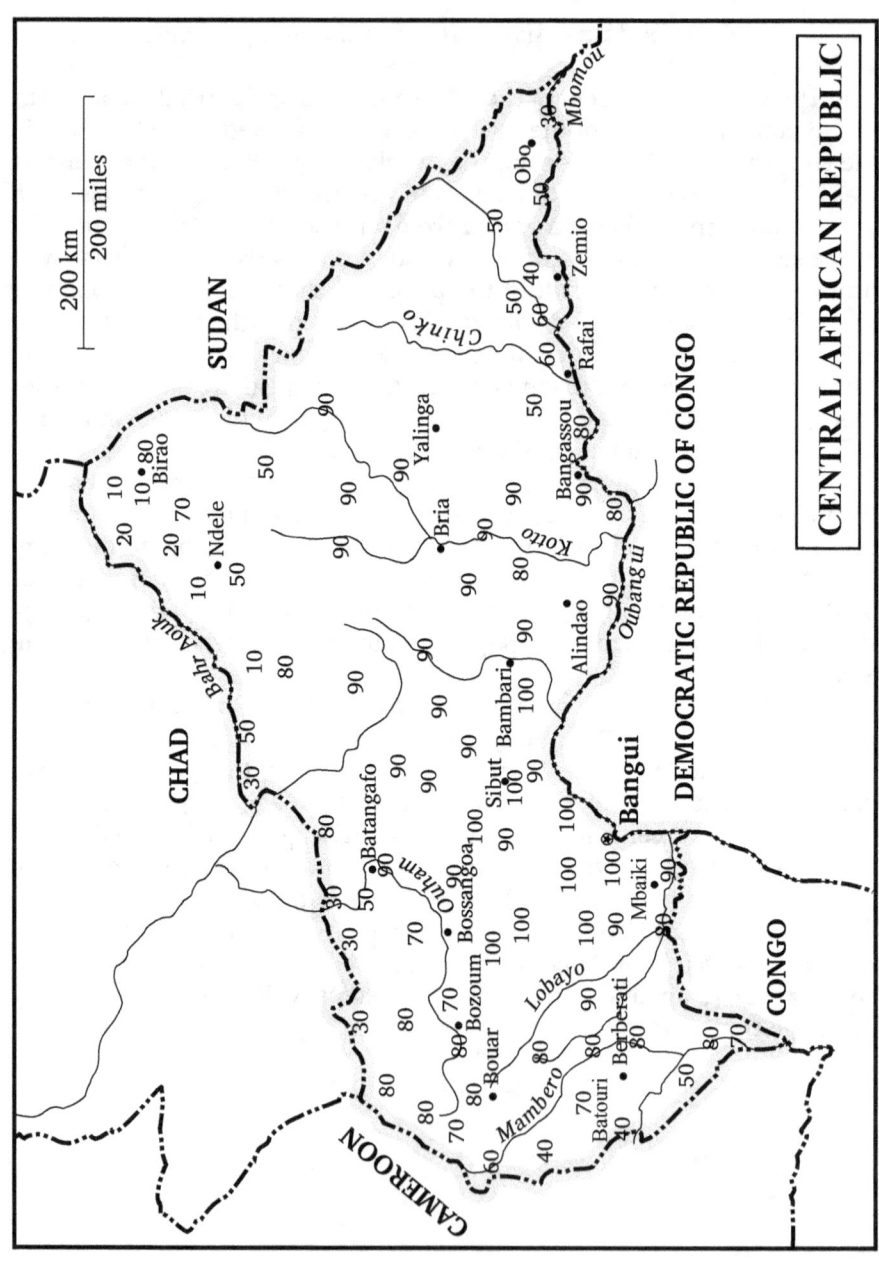

Figure 8.1 Percentage of Sango speakers per village

Census data—distribution of Sango speakers

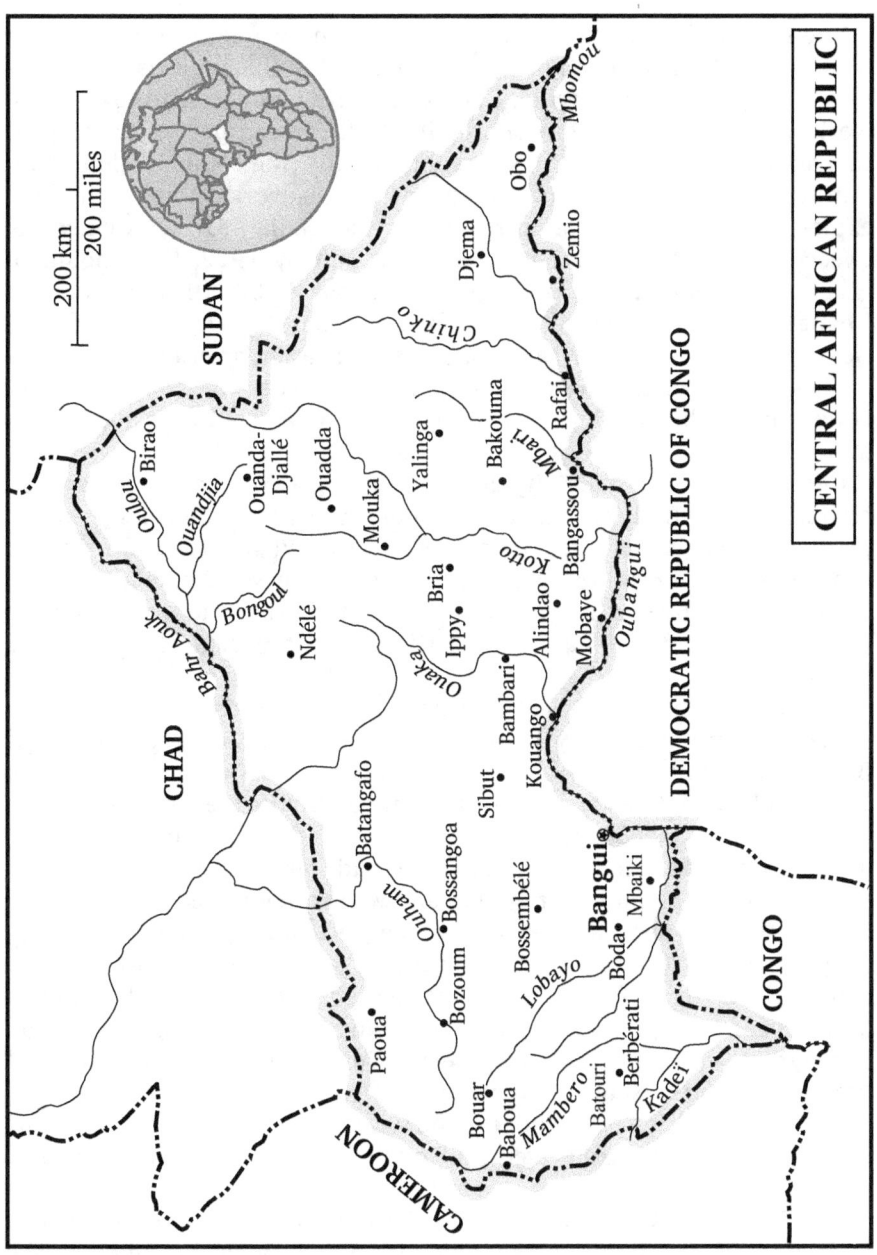

Figure 8.2 CAR map from The 1996 Grolier Multimedia Encyclopedia

The Ubangi (Oubangui) River was the main avenue of transportation (see figure 8.2). During all but the dry season the Ubangi is navigable between Bangui and Brazzaville, Congo, and provides access to the outside world via the rail link from Brazzaville to the ocean port of Point Noir. Gamandzori (1992:119–120) states that in 1899 the colonial administration requested that different private enterprises work on improving and exploiting the transportation route that the Ubangi River provided between Brazzaville and Bangui. He states that by 1912, the amount of cargo shipped in and out of Bangui was about 7,000 tons per year. The Ubangi is also navigable between Bangui and Bangassou. The Lobaye and Ouaka rivers were and are also main transportation arteries.

The regions which were in the past near the trade routes show a higher percentage of the population claiming to speak Sango. This is not surprising considering the history of the spread of Sango.

Church and mission activity also was often geographically determined by trade routes. Early church and mission activity is a factor in the spread of Sango. Two Protestant missions which started work around seventy years ago are the Brethren Mission and the Baptist Mid-Mission. Through an agreement, the Brethren Mission limited its work to the western part of the country, and the Baptist Mid-Mission to the central part of the country.

When the Baptist Mid-Mission first started working in the area, they made an administrative decision to work through the Sango language. Bruce Rosenau, an elderly Baptist Mid-Mission missionary who died in 1990, told me that his father, also a missionary in the area, told him of the decision to use only Sango for the ministries in the area. He said that the missionaries who came to start the work had some experience in present day Democratic Republic of Congo, and were discouraged by how many languages there were there and how the great number of different languages complicated the work. He stated that the decision to use only Sango was made to facilitate the mission work. Members of the Baptist Mid-Mission are proud of their contribution to the spread of Sango. Throughout the years, they have been involved in a lot of church-based literacy work in the Sango language.

The United Societies, in cooperation with the Brethren Mission and the Baptist Mid-Mission translated and published the Bible into Sango in 1966.

It is significant that the areas in which there was strong mission activity in Sango show the highest percentages of claimed Sango competence. The Baptist Mid-Mission had early works in the towns of Sibut, Ippy, Bambari, Ndélé, and Kaga Bandoro. The Brethren Mission had early works in the towns of Bouar, Bozoum, Bossangua, and Yalouke (near Bossembélé). These areas on the map in figure 8.1 show a very high percentage of Sango speakers. The spread of Sango was encouraged and facilitated by both trade and religious activities.

9

Observations and Conclusions

The spread of Sango

The distribution of the factors in the SRT analysis, as well as the interviews and observation, indicate that Sango is spreading at a fast rate. The positive side of this is that with more people speaking Sango, unity, communication, and education are facilitated in the country. A ramification of this, which is seen as negative by some, is that along with the spread of Sango there is a corresponding decline in the use of other languages.

Sango is moving somewhat into language domains and areas held in the past by French. However, in a much greater way, Sango is moving into language domains and areas held in the past by the ethnic group languages in the country. This implies a strong move toward the eventual abandonment of those ethnic group languages, a move which is already very evident in Bangui.

The character of language shift: individual based

In chapter 6, certain factors which were heavily weighted in predicting competence in Sango were discussed. Among these were age, schooling, and residence history. It is important to note that these factors are attributable to and individually influenced by individual people. Each culture has its young and old, its educated and noneducated, and so on. The fact that the strongest predictors of bilingualism are associated with individuals, and not with societies or groups (as are factors such as genetic distance, geographical distance), indicates that language spread is a function of individuals. The conglomerate of the individuals' behavior makes up the community behavior.

Using a regression analysis, with SRT results as the dependent variable, and using only factors that can be attributed to individuals, and not to groups, the amount of variation that can be accounted for by the factors of education, age, sex, occupation, residential history-Bangui, and residential history-large city is forty-seven percent (adjusted R squared): forty-seven percent of the variation of the SRT results is attributed to these individual-based factors! If I add to this the inherent differences in language aptitude to be found in individuals, the result is that, in large, predictors of language competence in a spreading language, and thus language shift, are based on factors associated with individuals.

Just as these individuals are shaped by the society, so also the society is shaped by the individuals. Individuals are not just stringed marionettes, jerked about by society. They are the very fabric and composition of society. Group behavior influences individuals, and individuals influence group behavior.

It is true that certain individuals have greater potential of influencing the society. Sometimes the smarter, or the industrious, or the stronger, or the better skilled, or better looking have greater potential of influencing society, but more often those privileged by birth have this greater potential.

We refer to the evils of a society and in doing so anthropomorphically attribute to a society the capacity to act and to deserve blame. Doing this, we divorce ourselves from the blame and responsibility of being a contributor to the pain and suffering found in the sectors of our society that we label needy. Even though attributing to society the power to act and deserve blame is necessary for our psychological denial, it is not conducive to a good understanding of language shift. People, some more influential than others, effectuate shift. Societies are the conglomerates of individuals who are very heterogeneous and individually motivated. There is often a similarity of motivations across a society, but with slightly different ramifications for different subsectors of the society.

Distribution of social correlates

We have seen in chapter 6 that the normal patterns of the distribution of social factors found in language change are also to be found in language shift. Individual-based factors, such as age, education, occupation, and sex pattern similarly. Interaction-based factors, such as the formality of the speech situation, also are similarly found. This gives credence to the view that language shift and language change are two reflexes of the same social process. This association of shift and change gives justification to the possibility that contributions from language change theory are applicable to language shift theory, and visa versa.

Language similarities and language shift

In chapter 7, we have seen that the degree of linguistic similarity between the language of the home and the spreading language did not function as a predictor of competence in the spreading language in this case. This could be peculiar to this particular situation, or could lead toward an understanding that the linguistic similarity between the languages in a language spread situation has less relevance than previously thought.

Motivations of language shift

I propose that there are a limited number of motivations active in language shift. They can be active on a conscious level or on a subconscious level. People may or may not be aware of the reasons behind their language choice decisions. All of the motivations involved in the choice of languages in particular situations can be grouped into a small number of classifications. These motivations are not just motivations of language choice, but are also the motivations that influence the acquisition of a language with the view to its future use in multilingual settings. I have grouped the motivations which are involved in language shift, into four types: communicative, economic, social (solidarity or prestige), and religious. Each is discussed below.

Communication

People make language code choices that will benefit communication. If your interlocutor does not know your primary language of communication, you will choose a different language held in common with the interlocutor, if one exists.

The best illustration is perhaps the extreme case example. If someone is shipwrecked onto a land where everyone speaks a language different from them, that person will quickly learn the language in order to be able to communicate. An exchange student jetted into the middle of country X will soon learn the local language. Many people in CAR have felt a need to know Sango in order to be able to communicate. As there are over forty languages spoken throughout the Central African Republic, and as Sango is the language of choice for inter-ethnic group communication, there is a strong and very realistic felt need to acquire and use Sango.

Economic gain

People make the code choice that they perceive will bring them the most fiscal gain. The importance of economic gain as a given factor in predicting shift was discussed. In chapter 8 the importance of economic motivations both in language choice decisions and in decisions on which language to teach offspring was reported. Parents and individuals make language code choices based on their perception of the economic ramification of those options.

In diglossic situations, where there is a functional difference between two languages in a community—a high and a low language—knowledge of the high language is almost always a prerequisite to obtaining the higher-paying jobs. Knowledge of the high language is usually a prerequisite to entry into the subsector of the community where wealth and potential wealth can be found.[10]

Social Advantage

This study found that getting ahead was often mentioned as a motivator of language shift. Parents spoke Sango to their children so that the children would be advantaged socially and economically. People considered Sango to be the language of advancement and prestige, without which one was a nobody.

Social advantage is the most commonly named factor in language shift and probably one of the strongest factors. In every culture, languages are attributed with differing degrees of prestige. Certain languages are associated with admired qualities, such as wealth, intelligence, technical superiority, sophistication, beauty, strength, power, and potency. Individuals choose to learn and speak these languages in order to be connected by association with these admired qualities, with the confirmed understanding that these qualities will also be attributed to them, in some measure, when they use the prestigious language. Use of the more prestigious language brings about gains in personal prestige.

---

[10]For further illustrations where economic gain is cited as a motivator of language shift, see Bentahila and Davies 1992, Trudgill and Tzavaras 1977, Paulston 1992, and Edwards 1985.

There are two basic types of social motivation for language choice: the social motivation that gives people the incentive to use the prestige language in a quest after power and prestige and influence, and the social motivation that calls for the use of an in-group language, which helps to bring about solidarity, unity, and acceptance. Although these two types of social motivations of language choice seem very different at first sight, there are actually close parallels between the two. In both types, the goal is association with positive qualities attributed to the languages in question. With the power type of social motivation, the positive qualities could be intelligence, technical superiority, sophistication, etc. With the solidarity type, the positive qualities could be friendliness, honesty, belonging to the neighborhood, acceptance, nonjudgmental attitude, straightforwardness, lack of pretension, good work ethics, and egalitarianism.

Both types of social motivation, power and solidarity, stem from a desire to be associated with positive characteristics which are associated with languages, but these positive characteristics are divided into two groups. In the one group are positive characteristics that are associated with power and prestige. In the other group are positive characteristics that are associated with friendliness and acceptance. In this respect, the choice between a high language and a low language can often be reduced to a choice between the social goal of gain through prestige and the social goal of gain through solidarity.

Religious motivations

Often there are languages that are associated with God or a god or a religion, and adherents would have a perceived religious benefit of using or learning that particular language. Sango, in the minds of some people, was connected to Christianity and God, while the ethnic mother-tongue languages were associated with the pagan religions.

There are many other examples, ranging from the use of Latin in the Roman Catholic Church, to the use of thee and thou in many Protestant churches in the United States and England, to the use of classical Arabic in the Islam world. Religion often is one of the motivators behind language code choices.

Mimicry

To the four motivations discussed above, I add the tendency toward mimicry that is an innate part of our language capacities, though one that declines with age. Mimicry can be seen as a social motivation, where speech conformity is a subconscious motivation because of the desire for solidarity or acceptance. However, I believe that it is more than that, that it is an important part of our language "hard wiring", a part that plays a large role in language shift and in language change.

Language loyalty

Language loyalty is a factor that must be included in any framework of language shift. It is a factor that comes into play when there is a perceived threat to one or more languages in a bi- or multi-lingual situation. In discussing language loyalty, Weinreich (1974:99–100) noted that language loyalty was a response to "impending language shift", and that "language loyalty breeds in contact situations just as nationalism breeds on ethnic borders." He also noted that language loyalty produces an "attempt at preserving the threatened language". Weinreich assumes that there is a fairly good attitude toward the threatened language. In cases where the shifting population holds a very low opinion of the threatened language, their original mother tongue, however, there are few signs of language loyalty and "attempts at preserving the threatened language". Further, language loyalty is a response to impending language death in a language shift situation, not impending shift, as stated by Weinreich. In general, people are unaware of impending shift.

Though language loyalty is a factor to consider, its effect is often not as strong as the other factors that influence language shift. Dorian (1982:47) maintains, "language loyalty exists as long as the economic and social circumstances are conducive to it, but if some other language proves to have greater value, a shift to that other language begins." In my evaluation, communicative, economic, social and religious motivations will all override language loyalties, but, at the same time, these loyalties are not to be ignored. Certain ramifications of language loyalty on language planning are discussed in chapter 10.

The SRT

Concerning testing devices to quantitatively study language competence and language shift, the SRT has proven to be a good tool. It is fairly simple to create. It gives reliable results. It is easy to administer to subjects. It does not require inordinate amounts of equipment. And it does not require a great deal of time to administer to each subject, thus allowing for the larger samples needed in quantitative study.

Summary

I maintain, therefore, that languages spread and shift occurs because individuals, consciously or subconsciously, make decisions to use certain languages in certain situations. These individual decisions are motivated by what each individual considers their personal good. People exploit and expand, and modify, their linguistic repertoires in order to gain perceived personal benefit. This benefit is either communicative, economic, social, or religious. When language spread or shift occurs, it does so because people choose to speak a different language for their own perceived benefit. Language shift and thus language death, does not "happen" to a community; rather, a community makes shift happen through individual choices motivated by a search for personal good.

Note that a key word is "perceived" in perceived benefit. The motivations that bring about language shift do not always bring about the reward that is hoped for. For example, when someone learns another language or switches to another language with the hope and motivation of economic benefit, there is not always economic gain. What motivates is the **perception** that that choice or acquisition of a language will bring about communicative or economic or social or religious benefit.

A community's behavior in a case of language shift can thus be considered the conglomerate of the individual decisions. Granted, group behavior plays a large part in what a community does, but from the individual motivation perspective, group behavior can be seen as individuals influenced by social motivations. The social motivations to use a particular language increase along with the number of people speaking that language. As more people choose to use a language, motivations for others to use that language increase.

Seeing language shift as a conglomerate of individual behaviors shaped by a limited number of motivations, reveals a surprising number of useful ramifications with important applications in the field of language planning and manipulation, especially in the areas of language maintenance and language death. The key to these ramifications is the focus on the motivations. Chapter 10 discusses a number of these ramifications.

10

Contributions to the Theory of Language Shift, Language Change, and Implications for Language Planners

The implications, observations, and ramifications presented in this chapter are based on the framework of language shift presented in chapter 9. Most of these implications, observations, and ramifications are only valid and relevant in light of an individual motivator's approach. In this framework, individuals making language choice decisions are central. The decisions themselves are made by each speaker seeking their personal communicative, economic, social, and religious good.

Inevitability of the continuation of language spread

The spread of languages of wider communication is a normal phenomenon. The most important implication for vernacular language development is probably the virtual inevitability of the spread of languages of wider communication.

In order to modify a shift situation, one must change the individual motivations that are bringing about the shift. In order to change those motivations, it is necessary to make drastic changes in the fabric of the society on which these motivations are based. It is a very complicated procedure to modify societal values and motivations. For example, in order to influence or modify economic motivations, drastic economic changes would be needed. Massive social and attitudinal changes would be needed to influence the social motivations. Mass programs of bilingualism among dominant neighboring populations would be needed to influence communicative motivations. And religious changes would be needed to influence religious motivations.

The enormity of these changes and programs naturally leads to a pessimistic conclusion concerning the preservation of endangered languages. When a shift is in progress, further shift is virtually inevitable. Edwards notes:

> Maintenance and revival efforts are usually artificial—in the sense that they are removed from a realistic overall appreciation of social dynamics—and doomed to failure. It is not surprising that they are initiated by persons atypical of those for whom they allegedly speak and that they usually fail to enlist the active support of the intended beneficiaries. (1985:169)

This is a strong statement but realistic in that many language preservation efforts are not working at the level of societal motivations that affect individuals.

Linguistic diversity, economics, and age of countries

Pool, in attempting to determine if there were any negative financial effects of multilingualism on a national level, discovered that "a country that is linguistically highly heterogeneous is always underdeveloped or semideveloped, and a country that is highly developed always has considerable language uniformity" (1972:221–222). This (negative) correlation seemed to imply that language heterogeneity was a cause of or a contributor to underdevelopment.

Coulmas, in his 1992 book entitled *Language and Economy* presents the statistics in table 10.1 to demonstrate the correlation between language heterogeneity and economic development. Study of this chart reveals the pattern of countries with high per capita incomes having low numbers of languages, and vice versa.

Table 10.1 Language heterogeneity and economic development
(Coulmas 1992:24)

Country	Population (Millions)	Per capita income ($)	Number of languages
Ethiopia	50	120 (1987)	120
France	56	16,090 (1988)	10
Vietnam	64	180 (1985)	77
Germany (FRG)	60	18,480 (1988)	7
Philippines	59	630 (1988)	164
UK	57	12,810 (1988)	7
Chad	5	160 (1987)	117
Denmark	5	18,450 (1988)	4
Benin	4.50	390 (1987)	52
Iceland	0.25	21,660 (1987)*	1
Bolivia	6	570 (1988)	38
Uruguay	3	2,470 (1988)	1
Indonesia	174	440 (1988)	659
Japan	122	21,020 (1988)	5
Sudan	23	480 (1988)	135
Netherlands	14.5	14,520 (1987)	5
Sweden	8	19,300 (1988)	5
Papua New Guinea	3.7	810 (1988)	849

*per capita GNP

Realizing that correlation does not imply causality, however, and in an attempt to find out if there were causative processes demonstrated in these type of data, Lieberson and Hansen (1974:536–537), used a multiple regressions correlation statistic in two separate studies and determined that no causal relationship could be demonstrated between linguistic diversity and the two measures of development that they used (literacy and urbanization). They determined, rather, that the negative correlation between linguistic diversity and development was due to two main categories of existing countries, old ones formed before World War II, and young ones formed after World War II. The countries that were formed before World War II were generally more developed and less diverse than those formed after the war. The countries formed after the war were, for the most part, linguistically diverse, nonindustrialized, former colonies who are disadvantaged in the development scheme by the somewhat monopolizing head start of the older countries.

The older countries are less linguistically diverse, and the younger countries are more linguistically diverse. Although again correlation does not imply causality, there is probably a causal relationship in that countries, over time, move toward linguistic homogeneity. This strongly implies that the spread of languages of wider communication at the expense of other languages is a natural, universal occurrence. An added implication is that one should not spend time and energy fighting against a natural process, but rather should take the process into consideration in all planning and execution of programs.

Governmental and institutional considerations

A second implication is that the governmental and institutional motivations that are contributing to the spread of languages of wider communication are real and strong. It is imperative that one recognize and use these existing motivations in any language-related programs. The results of ignoring these motivations are all negative: the programs will be reaching only people on the fringe of the society, the agents of change will basically be discounted as ignorant, there will be no real societal impact, and there will not be the local government cooperation that is needed for the success of most programs.

Also, ignoring peoples' motivations is basically ignoring their values, which does not build good relationships. Ignoring peoples' values is a typical characteristic of imperialism, and many countries in which language development programs are called for are sensitive about imperialism for obvious historical reasons. For example, a tendency to ignore peoples' values is strong when there are those who think a certain language should be preserved while the peoples' values and motivations are moving them away from this language with the full concurrence of the governments values and motivations.

Sometimes in language development or preservation projects initiated outside the country in which the project is to take place, there are considerations and perspectives held by governments and institutions in the country in question that are not adequately considered. There are many reasons why governments and institutions such as churches and development agencies favor the spread of a language of wider communication, which often results in policies which encourage the spread of these languages of wider communication, or discourage the use and development of vernaculars.

Communication in a multilingual country is often hindered, or at the very least complicated, by different languages among different sectors of the population. Governments and institutions can often see their communication problems resolved by the hope that their whole target population will use one language. Education, development, the political life of the country, and the bringing about of a democratic process, can all be simplified if the target population all understand a common language.

Language is one of the most important components of cultural identity. People identify with the social or cultural group associated with or represented by the language they are speaking. For this reason, in places where there is the possibility of a language of wider communication associated with the country, and where there is inter-ethnic-group strife or tension, governments and institutions will often strive to encourage the spread of this unifying language of wider communication.

In CAR, the government is very interested in encouraging the spread of Sango. They are interested in having the governmental, political, juridical, educational, and commercial aspects of life in CAR transacted in Sango. Recently, Sango was elevated to having official language status, along with French. There is a renewed desire to reintroduce Sango into the elementary schools and to have all aspects of government and commerce carried out in Sango.

When the geographical boundaries of CAR were arbitrarily set, they encompassed some groups who were traditional enemies. Inter-group jealousies, misunderstandings, stereotyping, and prejudice, though diminishing, are not uncommon. The government realizes that it must seriously consider that tribal warfare is a possibility and that they must do everything possible to prevent it from happening. One of the desires of the government is that people will see themselves less as members of an ethnic group and more as Central Africans. The government sees the development of Sango playing a major role in this change of viewpoint among the population(s). The philosophy is that when people are speaking Sango, they see themselves as belonging to the country and thus are more likely to put aside their inter-ethnic-group rivalries.

Thus, governments are often interested in the spread of languages of wider communication for communicative, educative and development reasons, and also for their value in uniting the country and helping bring about a national centered view of personal identity.

Religious groups are often supportive of the spread of languages of wider communication for the same reasons. Churches and missions working in CAR have been very supportive of the spread of Sango. In general, they see the Sango language as a blessing through which they can evangelize, teach, preach, and unite ethnic groups. Some of the churches and missions are proud of their historical part in the spread of Sango in the CAR. Some also see efforts to develop vernaculars as detrimental to the spread of Sango and detrimental to national or even church unity.

Groups involved in development work are also often favorable to the spread of languages of wider communication because of the way in which their lives and task are facilitated where there is a more national language of communication. Development workers in the CAR are generally appreciative of the possibilities of working through a language of wider communication—Sango, which can be understood by a large percentage of the people in the country. In general, they see the development of the country and the development of Sango going hand in hand.

The above mentioned perspectives and considerations held by governments and institutions often result in added support for the spreading language in a shift situation. There are many apparent advantages to a homogeneous linguistic situation. Thus, language preservationists, who maintain that endangered languages need to be preserved like endangered species, are figuratively trying to change the direction of a river by pumping water upstream, and could find themselves in a situation where the replacement parts that they need to keep their pump working end up "stuck" in customs. That is, they find themselves in situations where the needed components of support from the government are missing—inexplicably or wrongfully missing from their point of view.

Language planning through personal motivation modification

An implication that has already been mentioned is that if one desires to modify language shift trends, one must work on the level of personal motivations. It would be necessary to make language X more attractive and language Y less attractive by creating positive motivations toward language X and negative motivations toward language Y. Of the different motivations, social motivations are the easiest to manipulate.

In this discussion on modifying and manipulating motivation, however, it is necessary to realize how poorly placed outsiders are to attempt to modify societal values in this way. Even more so, outsiders are poorly placed to attempt to make value judgments on which programs would modify societal values.

Ways to encourage the spread of a language

In order to encourage the spread of a language, it is necessary to create the motivations that will bring about the choice of that language in language choice decisions. These same motivations will bring about a desire to learn the language for those who do not yet know the language.

Communication motivations

Communicative motivations could be increased by movements of population, by mass media, and by creating the desire and opportunity for a group to relate to a larger population.

Movements of population. Population movements can create situations where communication is impeded by the lack of a common language. In the CAR, Sango is the main language of the cities, because the cities' populations are composed of people from different ethnic groups. In this case, typical patterns of urbanization are encouraging the spread of Sango.

Another type of population movement, which has proven to be very effective, is that of moving government workers from one ethnic language area to a different ethnic language area on a regular basis. Doing so can assure more speech situations where there is a communication problem, thus motivating the acquisition of a more regional language. In these situations, the government workers, teachers, development agents, administrators, health workers, police, security, and military forces often are already using the language one desires to cause to spread.

In the CAR, government workers move on a regular basis, often every two years. They usually speak Sango in the workplace because of the multi-ethnic background of the workforce, and because it is the main language of Bangui, where most of them have received their training. The constant displacements of many government workers insure that they will, in general, end up using Sango and not the local vernacular of the place they are currently assigned. This constant displacement of government workers not only creates more communication situations where the spreading language must be used, it also sets up a social situation in the rural areas where those most likely to be the emulated role models of the youth are speaking the language one desires to cause to spread, adding a social motivation to the communicative motivation.

Mass media. Mass media, radio, television, and even literature, in a language one desires to cause to spread can be an effective means of increasing communicative motivations. This type of availability of desired information can motivate individuals to better learn the language in which the information is transmitted. In the CAR, there is, in general, a great interest in national and world politics. The national AM, FM, and Short Wave transmitters all broadcast the news in Sango on a regular basis throughout the day. The local television station in Bangui has a good deal of Sango programming and also broadcasts the news in Sango on a daily basis. My observation is that in the CAR, as compared to the USA, the news broadcasts are of more interest, are more listened to, or watched, and are more discussed by the population.

Desire to relate to a larger population. Another way to increase communicative motivations is to increase the desire of a person or population to relate to a wider community. The more attractive relating to a larger community is made to look, the more communicative motivations will be increased; the attractiveness is often financially based.

Financial motivations

These are among the strongest motivations in language shift situations and are often mixed with communicative and social motivations. When a language option is more attractive financially, it nearly always becomes more attractive socially. In the CAR, Sango has long been associated with financial benefit, first through its use as a language of trade between ethnic groups, and later because of its place in the post-colonial government where it is a prerequisite for good jobs and possibilities of financial gain.

In order to increase financial motivations among a population, in general, it is necessary to modify the financial base of the society. This is not easily done. There are, however, some actions and activities that have proven useful in increasing financial motivations to learn and use a language.

One effective tool is that of mandating proficiency in the language one desires to encourage for all government workers. In countries that are still on the road toward development, government jobs are often prestigious, much sought after, and relatively lucrative. Mandating proficiency in the language in question sends a strong signal that this language is associated with economic gain, and in a small way, can change the economic base of the country.

Another related motivation-increasing activity is making proficiency in the language in question a vital part of the formal education system. In most countries, education is highly related to financial success. Success in educational pursuits often brings about financial success, as well as accompanying social benefits. If proficiency in the language is made a vital part of the educational corpus, it can create an association between financial success and proficiency in the language. Other training in the language one desires to encourage can also create financial type of motivations by increasing the amount of money those who use the language can and do earn. Such training could be in agricultural methods, animal husbandry, small business operation, health precautions, (to help avoid the high costs of medicines and funerals), and various trades.

Development projects can also have a small impact on the financial basis of the country and thus slightly modify the basis and provide more financial motivation to learn and use a language. Farming co-operatives for marketing farm products can increase the relative wealth of those in the agricultural sector.

Social motivations

Social motivations are probably easier to create and manipulate than either communicative or economic motivations. Social motivations can be created by associating the language one wants to cause to spread with characteristics that are viewed as positive by the society. For instance, if the characteristic of independence is held in high esteem, associating a language with the characteristic of independence will create social motivations to use that language.

One simple way of creating social motivations to use a language is obtaining the cooperation of figures in the society who are highly respected, and having these figures use the language in question in public places and occasions. These figures could be politicians, sports figures, actors, millionaires, or others, provided that they are the people in whose shoes most of the population would like to be. The public places and occasions could be radio and television interviews, social events, official functions, and sports events. In this way the language is associated with socially prestigious people whom others would desire to emulate.

The association of a language with the concept of group solidarity is often a good manner in which to increase social motivations. The Sango language in the CAR is not only connected with the concept of national unity, it is actually being associated by some as connected with being a good, upright citizen because of the importance of group solidarity in that particular setting. A language that says "this is who we are, and we are part of a group we enjoy" will be a language that others are motivated to learn and use.

Religious motivations

In order to create religious motivations, it is necessary to form societal associations between religious good and the language in question. Religious motivations in general can be very powerful and are often critical motivating factors. In general, people see their religion as very positive. Associating a language with a religion by publishing religious books or having religious services in that language causes the association of that language with the positive aspects of the religion.

Ways to discourage the use of a language

There are three main ways to discourage the use of a language. The first of these is to provide motivation for learning and using a competing, spreading language of wider communication. The second is to provide negative motivations and decrease positive motivations toward using and learning the language one desires to discourage. And the third is elimination of the population speaking the language.[11]

As the first of these three methods—providing motivation for learning and using a competing, spreading language of wider communication—was discussed in the previous section and, as the third of these methods, genocide, is usually an ethnic rather than a linguistic matter, the discussion here is limited to the second of the three methods, i.e., providing negative motivations and decreasing positive motivations toward using and learning the language one desires to discourage.

Concerning communicative motivations, it is possible to communicatively devalue a language. One way of doing this is interdicting its use in government offices, with the result that there will be less motivation to use and learn that language due to fewer communication situations in which the language is of use. Another way is to decrease or eliminate mass media use of the language, which would decrease the communicative good found through the language.

Concerning economic motivations, the way to discourage the use of a language would be to economically devalue that language, that is, do

---

[11] I am not advocating discouraging the use of any language by any of the methods discussed. I present these methods simply to describe the processes used in the past, with the realization that these same processes may be used again in the future.

what is necessary so that the language will be of lesser or no use in finding economic good. If a knowledge of the language is necessary for any jobs, the prescribed action would be to modify those employments so that they would no longer necessitate, or even be facilitated by, a knowledge of the language. If there are programs of development or training in the language, the prescribed action would be to have those programs switch over to another language.

Concerning social motivations that would discourage the use of a language, it would be necessary to socially denigrate and disparage the language, attempting to set up associations between the language and characteristics that are unfavorable. This approach can be very effective. People would avoid using the language so that they are not associated with the negative characteristic or group. Associating the language of a post-colonial power with the evils of post-colonialism can create a situation where a choice of that language symbolizes sympathy with oppression, thus discouraging the use of the language.

One very common negative social characteristic associated with languages is that of being backward, uncivilized, or unenlightened. Generally, the most common scenario is where there is a social concept of a necessary social evolution from speaking the language in question to speaking another language. One man in the CAR, who thought that French was a superior language, when discussing literature in Sango, said with disdain, "Sango is for illiterates!" He was attempting to discourage the use of Sango by reinforcing an association between the Sango language and nonintellectuals. His use of the term "illiterate", to mean intellectually inferior, when used in this context of literature in Sango, turned his derision into a matter of mirth for those listening to him.

Concerning religious motivation the way to discourage the use of a language would be to create associations between the language and values that are stigmatized by the local religion. Since unity is highly valued in many religions, a possibly effective association could be between the language and ethnic separatism.

Implications concerning language loyalty

As mentioned in chapter 9, language loyalty results from the language and social identity of a group being threatened by a language shift, and often results in resistance to the shift. Attempts to discourage the use of a language, or to encourage the use of another, also can very easily incite resistance that comes from language loyalties.

In a bilingual community, language loyalty can be felt toward all the different languages in use, and may provoke resistance to programs focusing in on any one of the languages in a bilingual community. For instance, a monolingual development program in the language of wider communication of a bilingual community could develop resistance because the target group feels that their mother tongue is threatened. And a monolingual program in the mother tongue could develop resistance because the target group's desire to shift toward the language of wider communication could be threatened. The group might feel that there was an attempt to keep them as second-class citizens by keeping them monolingual in their mother tongue.

In the past, certain agents of change, desiring to encourage the spread of certain languages have done so by attempting to discourage the use of other languages. This has become an unwanted legacy to all who are now involved in language development. For many people, developing one language implies discouraging other languages. This implication is a contributing factor to language loyalty resistance. Because of these competing language loyalties in bilingual communities, those involved in language-related development should investigate the possibilities of programs of language development that have a multi-language aspect. For instance, if there is a program with the goal of increasing the percentage of the population that is literate in the Kaba language, and the Kaba people are motivated to learn to read Sango, even though they do not really speak Sango well, there will be more Kaba people reading Kaba after five years if the program is presented and designed to teach reading in both Kaba and Sango. If vernacular development programs include the languages that the people are shifting toward, there will be more likelihood of success.

Because of the complicating factors of language loyalty, and the resistance such loyalty can cause, it is extremely important to extend biliteracy concepts to the field of language planning and development. Biliteracy is basically reading and writing in two languages. Using the approach presented in chapter 9, in extending biliteracy concepts to language planning and development, it would be necessary to first analyze the language shift trends in a community, using a personal motivational analysis. This analysis would give insights into which languages the population was motivated to speak, and to desire to read. Then, these existing motivations can be used to help move the society toward group literacy in the languages indicated.

The key here is using the languages (PLURAL!) the community uses and is motivated to use and read. This approach would focus on literacy efforts that would move people toward group literateness in the languages that they were already motivated to use, thus overcoming the resistance to programs caused by language loyalty. With a biliteracy approach, a nonthreatening climate is created. A program to introduce Sango into the elementary schools in CAR failed because many parents thought their children would be disadvantaged by not learning in French. A biliteracy development approach could avoid this type of resistance.

Resistance caused by language loyalties brings several interesting implications:

If one desires to encourage the spread of a language of wider communication it could be disadvantageous to have monolingual programs in that language; the other languages of the community could be threatened. Conversely, bilingual programs can encourage the spread of a language of wider communication.

If one desires to encourage the spread or the maintenance of a vernacular, it could be disadvantageous to work only in the vernacular; loyalty to the other languages of the community could cause resistance to the program. Such a program risks appealing only to fringe members of the community. Conversely, bilingual programs can encourage the success of programs in the vernacular.

If one desires to encourage the death of a language, a good tool might be ineffectual monolingual "development" programs in that language that only appeal to fringe members of the society and have little societal impact. Such programs could help dissipate language loyalty toward the language one was trying to kill and thus help the shift toward other languages.

Recommendations for literacy work

It must be accepted that the spread of languages of wider communication is basically inevitable. Time and energy should not be wasted fighting against the inevitable. Programs should move toward a people (group) based approach, educating, helping, and reaching people groups through the languages the people choose to use. Programs should move away from a language-based approach, as such an approach can foster resistance caused by language loyalties. Literacy and other programs should not be frustrated by problems caused by resistance stemming from language loyalties.

After analyzing the language shift trends using a personal motivation type of analysis, the existing motivations should be used to help move the society toward group literacy in the languages they are choosing to use.

Implications concerning language change

One of the goals of this work was to see if the processes that are active in language change are also active in language shift. In chapter 3, numerous similarities between language change and language shift were discussed. In chapter 6, many of the patterns of the distribution of social factors were shown to be the same in both language shift as in language change.

This section looks at the implications and considerations drawn from the study of language shift to see if they are applicable to language change.

Language change can be viewed as a post-vernacular reorganization of the grammar; that is, it deals with the question of why people start to talk differently from their primary caregivers, a situation which takes place when language changes. "Post-vernacular" in this sense refers to a person's language changing after she or he has acquired the vernacular from their primary caregivers. "Reorganization" refers to the changes that occur in an individual's grammar when their language becomes different from that of their primary caregivers.

Because of the similarities between language shift and language change, applying the language shift framework, presented in chapter 9, to language change can be a natural step. Let us consider societal language change as the conglomerate of individuals involved in language change processes, motivated, either consciously or unconsciously, by the same motivations, as well as taking into consideration the mimicry factor. Let us consider, also, the possibility that language change occurs because individuals make decisions to use certain variants in certain situations, and that these individual decisions are motivated by what each one considers their personal good, whether a communicative, economic, social, or religious perceived benefit.

Paul (1880) in discussing language change, holds to the importance of the individual, stating that language usage can only be obtained by averaging individuals' mental language realities. Further, an individual's mental language reality is unique to the individual in form and development and is in a constant state of change. He also attributes the cause of changes in language usage to parallel changes in mental language realities, noting that the changes were parallel because of interpersonal interaction. His view is that there is a certain limited variability in production that may start a movement in a certain direction, depending on physiological ease or convenience; and that there is a psychological conditioning that influences how this variability moves toward a change in language custom.

Weinreich, Labov, and Herzog (1968) analyzed Paul's description of language change and observed that it was a bit lacking in that an averaging of individual use could be appropriate with a sound difference, but was meaningless with "soda and pop as two idiolectal designations of carbonated beverage...If the changes are nongradual, they can hardly yield to a 'summation'" (1968:106, 108).

Furthermore, Paul's view of physical ease being the motivating factor is lacking because it does not explain why some speakers experience sound change more quickly than others, and how and why one speech community splits into two or more separate communities through language change.

Thus, in a comparison of the ideas of Paul and those of Weinreich, Labov, and Herzog, there are two main issues, i.e., the domain of language usage or custom and the motivations of change.

Domain of language use or custom

Is the domain of language usage and custom the individual, or the group? If the domain of language custom were the individual, then there would have to be ideal individuals who had control of all of the different speech styles in a community. This is not the case. In communities with social stratification, certain individuals control certain styles and others other styles. Thus, the domain of language use and custom must be in some way the group, with some method of extracting the patterns of the individuals to make up group custom and usage.

It must be granted that language usage and custom do not exist outside of individuals. Individuals are of paramount importance, but they act together as a social organism. Paul's averaging concept is not sufficient in describing the true intricacies of this social organism which must include the structured heterogeneity of language that Weinreich, Labov, and Herzog support. Language is a social behavioral organism which acts on a societal level. At the same time, this organism is composed of individuals and groups of individuals, and the motivations that affect the group often operate on the individual level.

Language can be compared to a herd of animals. The herd is composed of individual animals which act in certain ways. There are distinctions in the herd distinguishable by different social factors. The older males are often on the periphery of the group to give protection. There are leaders who move the herd in a certain direction. There are certain animals on the fringe of the group. However, the herd often acts as one. It can spontaneously stampede, can have a disposition, and can move as one in a certain direction. A herd is a social organism, composed of individual organisms. To study a herd, it is imperative to consider both group behavior and individual motivations of the animals. When a herd moves toward better grazing or toward water, it is doing so because of hunger and thirst on the individual level. The direction the herd takes in seeking water or forage is based on a decision by one animal. But in this, the herd moves as one group.

In language change studies, it is necessary to see language as a social organism composed of individual organisms, and to consider both group behavior, and individual motivations when investigating how the community organism operates.

Motivations of change

Concerning the motivational issue, ease of pronunciation, as proposed by Paul, certainly has some effect on the direction of language change, but it is only one factor to be considered among many others. Sociolinguistic variables pattern differently in different socioeconomic classes. This patterning is not due to differences in the physiology of the members of the socioeconomic classes, but rather to how individuals react to socially conditioned motivations and patterns of use of the societal language organism. Different factors, with different amounts of impetus, influence individuals who make choices based on these factors. Thus, a factorial analysis on the level of the individual is appropriate in language change studies.

Language as a social organism

I see language as a social organism, composed of individuals. This composition is not an additive type of composition or an averaging. It is rather a composition of different parts making up a whole, as the different parts of a human body make up the whole body. In such a viewpoint, the characteristics of the individuals are critical to the understanding of the larger organism. The individual, as a component of the social organism of language, is motivated by societally based motivations that operate on an individual level.

This view of language also differs from the historical view of generative grammarians, who consider the individual to be the true domain of language (Chomsky 1965:3–4). The view presented in this work is based on a variationist perspective, acknowledging the importance of the socially structured heterogeneity of language. It also stresses the importance of the individual in motivational aspects, with the motivations themselves established on a societal level.

So, again, consider the possibility that language change occurs because individuals make decisions to use certain variants in certain situations. These decisions are motivated by what each individual considers will gain them personal perceived benefits, the motivations themselves formed by the larger society. Thus, language change on a societal level is the result of individual decisions.

Language acquisition process

In order to make this perception possible, it is also necessary to modify our understanding of the language acquisition process. One would have to adopt the view that the learner would be able to associate different variants of linguistic variables with certain people, certain classes of people, or certain values.

For example, a child from Philadelphia, learning the word "home" would not just learn the tag and the meaning, but would also learn there is fronting of the nucleus of the vowel diphthong in home—less fronting by certain older people, and more fronting by certain middle age people, and even more fronting by young people. In this way the child would be learning the variable along with associations of people or groups of people, or even concepts such as "youth", associated with certain variants (levels of fronting) of the variable. The child would also be learning that different variants are possibly associated with certain social distinctions. These could be categories of people which are geographically defined, age defined, class defined, or defined by other social factors. They could be associations between variants and concepts and ideas such as modern, good, popular, or lame.

Thus, the "orderly differentiation within language" (Weinreich, Labov, and Herzog 1968:151), that must be part of a full description of any language, is acquired by the new generation through this association of variables. Such a view of acquisition would allow us to consider language change in the model presented above for language shift. Such a view of acquisition would also rightfully predict an early acquisition and control of sociolinguistic variables, as well as early acquisition of distinctions such as men's talk and women's talk.

Assuming this view of acquisition, the child would be able to make choices, based on different motivations, of different variants in different situations. The child could be influenced by the social motivation of solidarity in choosing an advanced variant of a change-in-progress when talking to his or her peers because he or she realizes that that particular variant is associated with them or is associated with "young" and "popular" while the alternate variant is associated with "old fashioned". When speaking with his or her parents, the same child could chose a less advanced variant for the same solidarity motivation.

In a situation such as a school, the mimicry factor would also come into play, where an advanced variant would not only be used consistently because of its associations, but also because of simple mimicry.

As the child got older, other motivations could become active. The communication motivation could motivate the use of a conservative variant when communicating with an outsider or with an older person, where the advanced variant might lead to miscommunication. The economic motivation could also motivate the use of a conservative variant, when the individual was searching for a job and wanted to be seen as competent and mature and perhaps classy.

Labov's four problems

Labov (1995) presents four riddles or problems designed to facilitate the study of linguistic change in progress, or more specifically, post-vernacular reorganization. Labov's four problems are presented below along with my understanding of each.

1. The evolutionary problem. What is the adaptive mechanism that is the motivator in linguistic change?

With this viewpoint, the adaptive mechanism would ring a familiar bell. It would be the desire to survive, to better oneself, or to better compete with others. It would be the perception of personal gain (communicative, social, economic, religious) motivating the choice of the variant that would be perceived to best serve the speaker by bringing the perceived gain.

2. The uniformity problem. What factors bring about the uniformity that is present in speech communities despite the influx of new individuals with different speech systems?

Mimicry and the social motivation of solidarity would be active here. Acceptance is often gained through conformity. Certain phones and styles and variants and constructions would be associated with the societal norm. The social motivation of solidarity would encourage choices (conformity to the norm) that would be seen to best foster the acceptance desired.

3. The transmission problem. What is it that causes linguistic change to continue in the same direction over many generations?

In the acquisition description presented above, the learner would be associating different variants of sociolinguistic variables with different people, groups of people and with concepts and values. It would be this transmission of the association between the variants in a certain linguistic direction (e.g., fronting of vowels) with certain concepts and values that would allow changes to continue in the same direction over many generations. In acquisition, a learner would learn to associate, for example, fronting with young and modern and good, and a lack of fronting with old and stuffy and bad. This association would be passed on to the next generation through normal acquisition, allowing the change to continue on through generations with each generation fronting more than the last.

4. The completion problem. What is the motivational mechanism that would cause children to carry a change further than their predecessors, and on to completion?

The motivational mechanism here would be the association of advanced variants with positive values and concepts. The transmission of sociolinguistic variables would be through the transmission of values and concepts associated with certain directions of changes. In this model, children do not acquire sociolinguistic variables by attempting to mimic or emulate an older generation, but by making the choices of variants that would be perceived to bring about what was best for them, having acquired the association between advanced variants and positive values and concepts. Thus, the advanced variants could go beyond the discrete position of their parents' advanced variants because the process is not mimicry or emulation, but rather one of association of variants with values.

Conclusions

Concerning language change, observations that are helpful in understanding language shift and spread can be extended to language change. This model would seem to answer and resolve areas that were conundrums and problems in a different view of language acquisition and change.

The early control of sociolinguistic variables (purported by Roberts 1993) and male/female speech supports this viewpoint, in which variants are associated with individuals, groups, and then concepts and values early in the acquisition period. The manner in which this model facilitates the understanding of the transmission of sociolinguistic variables also argues for its acceptance. In this model, each and every speaker provides input in the acquisition of variables, as each speaker's variants are associated with his or her person, social factors and groups, and values.

Possible future studies, which would investigate the validity of the variant/value association, could be used to test the validity of this model e.g., a study of 12-year-old children in a situation where the vowel variables of different subsections of the society have been carefully mapped in different speech styles. The children would then be subjected to types of matched guise or association tests designed to determine if the children associate the different variants with different people, groups of people, or values.

This could be done by asking children to listen to a recording of an argument between a mother and her daughter and then asking them what the viewpoint of the mother was. The recording would be made to provide no clues as to which of the participants was the mother and which was the daughter, other than the linguistic clues of the speakers' vowels reflecting average vowel qualities for both adults and teenagers. Even the subject of the argument would be chosen so that it did not reflect typical inter-generational arguments thus giving no clue to who was who on the recording. It would be interesting to see what proportion of the subjects correctly identified the mother and then question the subjects on how they knew that person was the mother.

This type of test could reveal associations between variants of variables and age and authority. If the test did show a good degree of evidence of these associations, it could then be used to test younger and younger children, to see the age of formation of the association.

Finally, this study has shown that:

1. The Sentence Repetition Test is a good tool for quantitative study of language shift, using competence in the spreading language as an indicator of language use.
2. Social factors are good predictors of competence in a spreading language while language genetic factors were not good predictors in the case studied.
3. Language shift and language spread are best studied from a perspective that investigates individuals' motivations for language choice and for language acquisition.
4. The motivations in question can be classified into the categories of communicative, economic, social, and religious.
5. The individual motivation framework of language spread is well-suited to understanding and influencing language spread and language maintenance.

6. There are many similarities between language shift and language change. It is possible that they are indeed manifestations of the same process. If this is the case, children's language cognition would include associations between variants of sociolinguistic variables and societal classifications and values. This is a testable hypothesis.

Appendix 1

Interlinear Texts

1. *mbï gue na yäkä*
   1PS aller au champ
   Je vais au champ.

2. *lo yeke kä nyama na galã*
   3PS être vendre animal au marché
   Il vend de la viande au marché.

3. *babã a-gue na ngû ti gi susu*
   père Ø-aller à eau pour chercher poisson
   Papa est parti à la rivière pour pécher des poisson.

4. *gïgï ti fadësô ayeke ngangû mingi*
   monde de maintenant être difficile beaucoup
   La vie d'aujourd'hui est très difficile.

5. *ë yeke gue tî sukûla ngû na bale*
   nous être aller pour laver eau au fleuve
   Nous allons nous baigner au fleuve.

6. *môlengê tî wâlï sô a-kpa mamâ tî lo mîngi*
   enfant de femme ce Ø-ressembler mère de 3PS beaucoup
   Cette fille ressemble beaucoup à sa mère.

7. lo   yeke fa   terê   tî lo mîngi
   3PS être montrer corps de 3PS beaucoup
   Il se vante beaucoup.

8. gue   mo tö   ngû mo gä   na   ni   mbï nyön
   aller 2PS est eau 2PS venir   avec en.question 1PS boire
   Va m'apporter de l'eau à boire.

9. â- môlengé a-yeke   so   ka   li   ti zo
   pl enfant Ø-être   souffrir habituellement tête de personne

   mingi
   beaucoup
   Les enfants sont généralement très embêtants.

10. ë   yeke gue   tî   sâra   ngiâ na   da   tî dödö
    nous être aller pour faire joie dans maison de danse
    Nous allons nous distraire au dancing.

11. kôlï   sô a-yê   mingi   tî dîko â-mbëtï tî sängö
    homme ce Ø-aimer beaucoup de lire pl-livre de sängö
    Cet homme aime lire les livres écrits en sängö.

12. mamâ sô a-yeke sâra ka   â-yê   tî ngiâ
    mère ce Ø-être faire habituellement pl-chose de joie

    mingi
    beaucoup
    Cette dame fait habituellement des choses très drôles.

13. dütingö   tî kôlï   na   wâlï   a-nzere na   papa
    action.d'être   de homme avec femme Ø-bon   avec querelle

    pëpëe
    ne...pas
    Les querelles ne sont pas bonnes pour une vie de couple.

14. tî   Tekue nyöngö   sâmba   ni
    pour   Tekue action.de.boire boisson.alcoolique en.question

```
            a-bön         ndö    ní              awe
            Ø-dépasser    dessus en.question     déjà
            La consommation de boissons alcoolisées est exagéres chez Tekue.
```

15. lo yeke sû   mbëtï tï   tokua   na yayâ tï lo   na Amerika
    3PS être écrire livre pour envoyer   à l'ainé de 3PS en ***
    Il rédige une lettre pour envoyer à son ainé en Amérique.

16. mbï baâ mbênî   pendere wâlï   sô a-yeke hön   kâ   na
    1PS voir un.certain belle   femme   qui Ø-être passer   là.bas sur

    lêgë
    route
    Je vois passer, làbas, sur la route, une belle femme.

17. lâsô   mamâ a-tö   koko   na   nyama
    aujourd'hui mère Ø-est sorte.de.feuille avec animal
    Maman a préparé aujourd'hui du koko au nyama.

18. kôya   a-fâ   bîrï â- makâko ûse na   ngombe
    oncle.maternel Ø-circoncier hier pl singe 2   avec fusils
    Mon oncle maternel a tué, hier, au fusils, deux singes.

19. wâlï   sô a-yeke längö ndürü na teré   tï da   tï mbï
    femme   ce Ø-être jour près de corps de maison   de 1PS
    Cette femme dort près de ma maison.

20. mamâ a-sâra pendere pëtë   na   li   tï ngambe tï mbï tï
    mère Ø-faire belle tresse sur tête de cadette de 1PS de

    wâlï
    femme
    Maman a fait une belle tresse à ma petite soeur.

21. lâ   a-su   mîngi   na yâ   ti â-längö sô sï
    soleil Ø-briller beaucoup en intérieur de pl-jour ce et

    â-kôbe   tï yäkä kûê   a-buba
    pl-nourriture de champ toutes Ø-gâcher
    Il y'a eu tant de soleil ces jours ci que tous les produits champêtres ont été détruits.

22. â- wagïngö   nyama   a-fâ   lâsö   mbêni   kötä
    pl chercheur animal Ø-circoncier   aujourd'hui un.certain grand

   kûma sô   lo   mene   â-kêtê   uga   ûse
   boa qui 3PS avaler pl-petit biche 2
   Les chasseurs ont tué, aujourd'hui, un boa qui a avaler deux petites.

23. tî   tene   mo hînga   nzërëngö tî kundä a-yeke nzönî a-tö
    pour parler 2PS connaitre   goût   de tortue Ø-être bon   Ø-est

   lo   na   kpë tî sindi   ngâ   na   karakanzi sï
   3PS avec pâte de sésame   aussi avec ***   d'abord
   Pour apprécier le goût de la tortue, il faudrait la préparer avec la
   pâte de césame et du karakanzi.

24. wálï   tî   mbï a-lü   nzö   na   â- kugbê   tî kâsa
    femme de   1PS Ø-planter   maïs   avec pl sorte.de.feuille   de sauce

   mîngi   mîngi   na terê   tî   da   tî   ë
   beaucoup beaucoup â   corps   de   maison de   nous
   Ma femme a planté du maïs et beaucoup de légumes près de notre
   maison.

25. kötarä   a-yeke fâ   â-këkë   na   yâ   tî   yäkä   tî
    ancêtre   Ø-être circoncier   pl-arbre dans   intérieur de   champ de

   fondo   tî   lo
   bananes.plantains de   3PS
   Grand-père abat les arbres dans son bananeraie.

   yê   ôko na   tïngö   tî   â-këkë   nî   âla
   chose   1   en   action.de.tomber de   pl-arbre   en.question   3PP

   kûngbi   â-mbênî   fondo   nî
   casser   pl-un.certain   bananes.plantains en.question-pl

   mîngi   na sêsê
   beaucoup â   terre
   Seulement, en tombant, ces arbres ont térrassé certains bananiers.

26. na bï   sô â-gbâ   tî   â-bobo   a-sïgïgï na gbe   tî   wâ na
    en nuit ce pl-tas   de-pl   termites Ø-sortir da dessous de   feu au

   yângâ   tî   lëgë
   bouche de   chemin
   Cette nuit beaucoup de termites sont sorties sous les lampadaires sur la route.

27. töngana mo   kpë   kötä   zo   fadë   gïgï tî mo   a-gue
    comme   2PS respecter grand personne (futur) vie de 2PS Ø-s'en

   a-yo
   Ø-être
   Si tu respectes les personnes âgées, tu vivras longtemps.

28. lo   de   môlengê mingi   nî.laâ   lo   ngbá   tî sâra
    3PS rester enfant   beaucoup c.est.pourquoi   3PS rester de faire

   â-yê   tî kîrîkiri   sô
   pl-chose de desordre   ce
   IL est encore très jeune, c'est pourquoi el agit d'une manière irréfléchie.

29. a-dü   mamâ   kêtê   tî   mbï na ngû   sâke   ôko ngbangbo
    Ø-enfanter   mère   petit   de   1PS en année   mille 1   100

   gümbâyä na   balë okü na   ndünî   mbârâmbârâ
   9   et   10   5   et   dessus   7
   Ma jeune tante maternelle est née en 1957.

30. wâlï   tî   Bagaza   a-lï   yâ   tî   pendere bongo tî   lo
    femme   de   ***   Ø-entrer   intérieur   de   beau   habit de   3PS

   tî   gue   na   nî   na   da   tî   Nzapä
   pour aller   avec en.question   dans   maison de   Dieu
   La femme de Bagaza a mis sa belle tenue pour se rendre à l'eglise.

31. ge   tî   güengö   na   kötä   lêgë   a-yo   a-lîngbi
    ici   pour action.de.partir   sur grand chemin   Ø-être   Ø-convenir

ndurü na kilomètre balë mbârâmbârâ na ndö nî
près de *** 10 7 avec dessus en.question

mbârâmbârâ
7
D'icia la grande route, il faut compter â peu prés soixante et dix-sept kilomètres.

32. *mbênî bîrï na bï â-zo tî Bimbo a-pîka*
un-certain hier dans nuit pl-personne de *** Ø-battre

ngo sï âla dödö ngbii a-sï na ndâpêrêrê
grossesse et dans longtemps Ø-arriver au matin
Hier nuit, les habitants de Bimbo ont joué du tam-tam et ont dansé jusqu'au matin.

33. *mängö terê na yâ tî küdürü laâ a-sâra sï*
fait.d'écouter corps dans intérieur de village cela Ø-faire que

küdürü a-gue na ndüzü
village Ø-aller en ciel
L'entente dans un pays fait que ce pays de développe.

34. *a-gbû mbênî zo tî nzï na bï sû sï a-pika lo*
Ø-attraper un.certain personne de vol en nuii ce et Ø-batire 3PS

ndürü na kûâ
prés de mort
Un voleur a été attrapé et battu jusqu'a l'agonie, cette muit.

35. *môlengê tî kossi a-yo a-hön lo tî Befio ata sô*
enfant de *** Ø-être Ø-cépasser 3PS de *** Même que

ngû tî âla a-lîngbi terê
année de 3PP Ø-convenir corps
L'enfant de kossi est plus grand que celui de Befio même e'ils ont le même âge.

36. *â- zo tî Bêafrika a-ngbâ tî längö na da tî*
pl personne de *** Ø-rester de jour dans maison de

pêrë
paille.pour.couvrir.un.toit
Les centrafricains continuent d'habiter les maisons en paille.

37. *lâkûê   na lâpôsô Dambalé a-yeke tene   ka   tere*
    toujours â   samedi ***   Ø-être parler habitueliement conte

    na yâ   tî fonônö
    dans intérieur de radio
    Tous les samedi, Dambalé présente des contes â la radio.

38. *kôgarä   tî mbï tî wâli   a-tokua   bírï mbëtï tî fa*
    belle.mère de 1PS de femme Ø-envoyer hier livre de montrer

    längö tî gängö tî lo na   ndo tî ë
    jour   de venue de 3PS chez lieu de nous
    Hier, ma belle mère a envoyé une lettre pour nous indiquer la date de sa visite chez nous.

39. *kôlï   sô a-yeke siönî   mingi   ngbanga tî sô lo yeke*
    homme   ce Ø-être mauvais beaucoup parce   de ce 3PS être

    pika   ka   wâlï   tî lo na â-môlengê tî lo
    batire habituellement femme   de 3PS et pl-enfant de 3PS

    lâkûê   lâkûê
    toujours toujours
    Cet homme est très mauvais car il bat tourjours sa femme et ses enfants.

40. *kua   tî ndao   a-yeke ngangü kua   mîngi*
    travail de forgeron Ø-être difficile travail beaucoup
    Le metier de forgeron est très difficile,

    töngana mo yeke kôlï   pëpëe   mo lîngbi   tî sâra
    comme   2PS être homme ne...pas 2PS être.capable de faire

    nî   pëpëe
    en.question ne...pas
    Si tu n'est pas un homme, tu ne peux le faire.

Appendix 2:
RPE Proficiency Evaluations Wording

Descriptions pour l'évaluation des compétences dans le domaine de l'accent

A. Souvent les gens ne comprennent pas ce qu'il dit parce que sa prononciation est très mauvaise.

B. Les gens ont de la peine à le comprendre parce qu'il fait souvent de grosses erreurs de prononciation et qu'il a un accent très fort. Les gens lui demandent toujours à nouveau de répeter ce qu'il a dit.

C. Les gens doivent l'écouter avec attention parce qu'il parle le sängö avec l'accent de sa langue maternelle.

D. Les gens peuvent facilement le comprendre, même avec des errours de prononciation et son accent prononcé.

E. Même s'il ne fait pas d'erreurs évidentes de prononciation, il a cependant un léger accent.

F. Sa prononciation et son accent sont parfaits.

Descriptions pour l'évaluation des compétences dans le domaine de la grammaire

A. La grammaire est presque toujours inexacte, sauf dans les phrases qu'il a apprises par coeur ou celles qu'il utilise fréquemment.

B. Souvent les gens ne comprennent pas ce qu'il veut dire à cause de ses erreurs grammaticales.

C. Il fait fréquemment des erreurs qui irritent quelquefois les autres et occasionnent aussi des malentendus.

D. Il fait souvent les même erreurs grammaticales. Cependant, les gens le comprennent toujours.

E. Pas de lacunes évidents. Il fait très peu d'erreurs grammaticales.

F. Même lors d'une longue conversation, il ne fait qu'une ou deux erreurs, si encore il en fait.

Descriptions pour l'évaluation des compétences dans le domaine de facilité d'élocution

A. Une conversation avec cette personne est pratiquement impossible parce que ses phrases sont tellement hésitantes et décousues.

B. Il parle toujours très lentement, s'arrête puis recommence fréquemment, sauf pour les phrases courtes et routinières.

C. Il s'exprime souvent avec beaucoup d'hésitation. Il ralentit fréquemment son discours et quelquefois il ne peut pas finir ses phrases.

D. Il hésite quelquefois quand il parle. Son discours est parfois irrégulier parce qu'il essaie de se remémorer un mot ou essaie de reformuler sa phrase.

E. Il parle couramment et sans difficulté, mais à cause d'une légère irrégularité dans le rythme, les gens peuvent dire que le sängö n'est pas sa langue maternelle.

F. Peu importe le sujet de la comversation, que ce soit d'ordre général ou spécifique, son discours est aussi rapide et régulier que celui d'un locuteur de langue maternelle sängö.

Descriptions pour l'évaluation des compétences dans le domaine de vocabulaire

A. Même dans la conversation la plus simple, cette personne éprouve des difficultés, parce qu'il y a trop de mots qu'elle ne connaît pas.

B. Il connaît juste assez de mots pour parler de choses personnelles et vitales telles que famille, temps, déplacements, voyages et nourriture.

C. Il a assez de vocabulaire pour parler de sujets quotidiens tels que travail ou autres bavardages. Il utilise parfois le mauvais mot parce qu'il ne connaît pas le mot exact. Son vocabulaire limité l'empêche d'entrer dans quelques discussions d'ordre professionels ou sociaux.

D. Son vocabulaire est généralement suffisant pour parler de tous les sujets d'ordre général. Parfois il doit expliquer ce qu'il veut dire parce qu'il ne connaît pas le mot exact. Il peut parler facilement de son propre travail et de tout ce qui l'intèresse parce qu'il connaît tous les mots particuliers qui y ont trait.

E. Il connait tous les mots relatifs à son travail et à ses centre d'intérêts et il est toujours capable de choisir le mot exact dont il a besoin. Il a suffisamment de vocabulaire pour parler de choses compliquées ou inattendues qui se présentent dans des situations sociales diverses.

F. Son vocabulaire est aussi étendu et précis que celui d'un locuteur de langue maternelle sängö; il utilise toujours le mot exact, à tel point que personne ne remarque que le sängö n'est pas sa langue maternelle.

Descriptions pour l'évaluation des compétences dans le domaine de compréhension

A. Lorsque les gens lui parlent en sängö, il comprend si peu qu'il est impossible d'avoir une conversation avec lui.

B. Il comprend seulement une conversation très lente et simple ainsi que les phrases usuelles pour voyager, acheter et vendre. Pour qu'il comprenne ce qu'on lui dit, il faut toujours qu'on lui répète les phrases ou qu'on les reformule avec des mots plus simples.

C. Il peut comprendre un discours en sängö si les gens lui parlent distinctement, mais ils doivent souvent répéter des phrases ou les reformuler plus simplement.

D. Il comprend généralement les gens même s'ils ne font pas spécialement attention ou ne parlent pas spécialement lentement, mais parfois il ne comprend pas et les gens doivent répéter ou reformuler leurs phrases.

E. Lorsqu'il parle avec des locuteurs de langue sängö, il comprend tout, sauf les mots extrêmement rares, les mots d'argot, ou encore un discours très rapide ou mal articulé.

F. Il comprend tout aussi bien qu'un locuteur de langue maternelle sängö, que ce soit un sujet général ou spécifique, un language formel ou familier.

Appendix 3

Second Language Proficiency Levels Descriptions[12]

RPE level 0+. Very minimal proficiency.

RPE level 1. Minimal, limited proficiency.

> A person at this level has a very heavy accent which makes understanding difficult and forces people to ask for repetition. There seem to be more mistakes in grammar than correct usage, except for stock phrases. Vocabulary is limited to basic personal and survival areas. Speech is slow and halting except for short or routine sentences. Understanding is limited to slow, very simple speech, with very frequent repetition and rephrasing.

RPE level 1+. Limited, basic proficiency.

RPE level 2. Adequate, basic proficiency.

> A person at this level has a heavy accent that forces people to concentrate when listening and sometimes causes misunderstanding and gives the appearance of errors. Some important grammatical rules are not controlled which occasionally causes misunderstanding and even irritation. Vocabulary is broad enough for daily topics, but limited in some common domains and sometimes inaccurate. Hesitations and jerkiness are frequent. Sometimes sentences cannot be completed. Understanding is possible if people speak carefully and simplify their speech somewhat, but they must repeat and/or rephrase frequently.

---

[12]Quoted from Radloff (1991:137–138).

RPE level 2+. Good, basic proficiency.

RPE level 3. Good, general proficiency.

A person at this stage has a marked "foreign" accent, with occasional mispronunciations, but these do not interfere with understanding. Imperfect control of some grammatical patterns causes occasional errors, but understanding is not affected. Vocabulary is adequate to cope with varied social situations and special interests in professional domains with some circumlocutions. Speech is occasionally hesitant and perceptibly nonnative in speed and evenness. Normal educated speech is understood quite well, with only occasional need for repetition or rephrasing.

RPE level 3+. Very good, general proficiency.

RPE level 4. Excellent proficiency.

A person at this level still has a very slight accent but no longer mispronounces words. No patterns of grammatical error remain and only rarely are errors made. Vocabulary is broad and precise, adequate for all technical, social, and practical situations. Only a slight difference in the speed and evenness of speech separates this speaker from a native speaker. Comprehension is complete except for very slurred or rapid speech or perhaps uncommon words or idioms.

RPE level 4+. Approaching native speaker proficiency.

Appendix 4
Individual Subject SRT Scoring Sheet

Nom: Addr: No:
Age: Sexe: L Mat: L Foy: L Trv: Mét:
L ED: NvEd: L Mère: L Père: L Époux/se:
Adm: Tech: Date: Ref:

Endroits où il a séjourné pendant plus d'un an
         endroit   durée   quand
1.
2.
3.
4.
5.

Teste de Bilinguisme en Sango - SRT

P1. Mbï gue na yäkä.

P2. Lo yeke kä nyama na galâ.

1. Lâsô mamâ atö koko na nyama.
2. Gïgï tî fadësô ayeke ngangû mîngi.

3. Âzo tî Bêafrika angbâ tî längö na da tî pêrë.
4. Ë yeke gue tî sâra ngîâ na da tî dödö.
5. Agbû mbênî zo tî nzï na bï sô sï apîka lo ndürü na kûâ.
6. Wâlï sô ayeke du ka na kötä bê mîngi.
7. Mamâ asâra pendere pëtë na li tî ngambe tî mbï tî wâlï.
8. Maseka sô ayeke he ka bîâ nzônî mîngi.
9. Wâlï tî Bagaza ayü pendere bongo tî lo tî gue na nî na da tî Nzapä.
10. Lo de môlengê mîngi nî laâ lo yeke sâra yê tî kîrîkiri sô.
11. Môlengê tî kossi ayo ahön lo tî Befio, ata sô ngû tî âla alïngbi terê.
12. Kôgarä tî mbï tî wâlï atokua bîrï mbëtï tî fa längö tî gängö tî lo na ndo tî ë.
13. Tî tene mo hînga nzërëngö tî kundâ, ayeke nzönî atö lo na kpë tî sindi ngâ na karakanzi sï.
14. Ge tî guengö na kötä lêgë ayo alîngbi ndurü na kilomêtre balë mbârâmbârâ na ndö nî mbârâmbârâ.
15. Âwagïngö nyama afâ lâsô mbênî kötä kûma sô lo mene âkêtê uga ûse.

References

Ash, Sharon. 1982. The vocalization of /L/ in Philadelphia. Ph.D. dissertation. University of Pennsylvania.

Bailey, Charles-James N. 1973. Variation and linguistic theory. Washington, D.C.: Georgetown University Press.

Baker, Colin. 1992. Attitudes and language. Clevedon, Philadelphia, and Adelaide: Multilingual Matters LTD.

Bamgboṣe, Ayọ. 1991. Language and the nation: The language question in sub-saharan Africa. Edinburgh University Press.

Baratz, Joan C. 1969. Teaching reading in an urban Negro school system. In Joan Baratz and Roger Shuy (eds.), Teaching black children to read, 92–116. Washington, D.C.: Center for Applied Linguistics

Bentahila, Abdelâi, and Eirlys E. Davies. 1992. In Willem Fase, Koen Jaspaert, and Sjaak Kroon (eds.), Maintenance and loss of minority languages, 197–210. Amsterdam and Philadelphia: John Benjamins.

Bickerton, Dereck. 1973. The nature of a creole continuum. Language 49:640–669.

Bouquiaux, Luc, Jean-Marie Kobozo, and Marcel Diki-Kidiri. 1978. Dictionaire sango-français (Centrafrique). Paris: SELAF (Tradition Orale, 29).

Bourdieu, Pierre. 1982. Ce que parler veut dire: L'économie des échanges linguistiques. Paris: Fayard.

Bourdieu, Pierre. 1987. Choses dites. Paris: Editions de Minuit.

Bourdieu, Pierre, and Luc Boltanski. 1975. Le fétichisme de la langue. Actes de la recherche en sceinces sociales 4:2–32.

Brown, Roger and Albert Gilman. 1960. The pronouns of power and solidarity. In Thomas A. Sebeok (ed.), Style in language, 253–276. Cambridge, Mass.: Technology Press of MIT. (Reprinted in Pier Paolo Giglioli, ed. 1972. Language and social context, 252–282. Harmondsworth: Penguin Books.)

Brudner, Lilyan. 1972. The maintenance of bilingualism in Southern Austria. Ethnology 11(1):39–54.

Callary, R. E. 1975. Phonological change and the development of an urban dialect in Illinois. Language in Society 4:155–170.

Cobarrubias, Juan, and Joshua Fishman, eds. 1983. Progress in language planning. The Hague: Mouton.

Cooper, Robert L. 1989. Language planning and social change. Cambridge, UK and New York: Cambridge University Press.

Coulmas, Florian. 1992. Language and economy. Oxford, U.K. and Cambridge, Mass.: Blackwell.

Couvert, Claude. 1983. La langue française en République Centrafricaine. Paris: I.R.A.F.

Data Desk 4.1. 1993. Ithaca, N.Y.: Data Descriptions, Inc.

Diki-Kidiri, Marcel. 1977. Le sango s'écrit aussi... Esquisse linguistique du sango, langue nationale de l'Empire Centrafricain. Paris: SELAF (Traditions Orale 24).

Dorian, Nancy. 1982. Language loss and maintenance in language contact situations. In Richard D. Lambert and Barbara F. Freed (eds.), The loss of language skills. Rowley, Massachusetts: Newbury House.

Educational Testing Service. 1970. Manual for Peace Corps language testers. Princeton, N.J.: ETS.

Edwards, Anthony D. 1976. Language in culture and class: The sociology of language and education. London: Heinemann.

Edwards, John. 1985. Language, society and identity. Oxford and New York: Basil Blackwell.

Fase, Willem, Koen Jaspaert, and Sjaak Kroon. 1992. Maintenance and loss of minority languages: Introductory remarks. In Willem Fase, Koen Jaspaert, and Sjaak Kroon (eds.), Maintenance and loss of minority languages, 3–13. Amsterdam and Philadelphia: John Benjamins.

Fasold, Ralph. 1984. The sociolinguistics of society. Oxford: Basil Blackwell.

Fishman, Joshua. 1964. Language maintenance and language shift as fields of inquiry. Linguistics 9:32–70.

Fishman, Joshua. 1965. Who speaks what language to whom and when? Linguistics 2:67–88.

Fishman, Joshua, ed. 1968a. Readings in the sociology of language. The Hague: Mouton.

Fishman, Joshua. 1968b. Sociolinguistic perspective on the study of bilingualism. Linguistics 39:21–49.
Fishman, Joshua, ed. 1972a. Advances in the sociology of language, vol. 2. The Hague: Mouton.
Fishman, Joshua. 1972b. Domains and the relationship between micro- and macro-sociolinguistics. In Gumperz and Hymes 1972, 435–453.
Fishman, Joshua. 1972c. The relationship between micro- and macro-sociolinguistics in the study of who speaks what to whom and when. In J. B. Pride and Janet Holmes (eds.), Sociolinguistics, 15–32. Harmondsworth: Penguin.
Fishman, Joshua. 1984. Studies of language as an aspect of ethnicity and nationalism, (bibliographic introduction). Sociolinguistics Newsletter 14(2):1–6.
Fraser, C., Ursula Bellugi, and Roger Brown. 1963. Control of grammar in imitation, comprehension, and production. Journal of Verbal Learning and Verbal Behavior 2:121–135.
Gal, Susan. 1978. Variation and change in patterns of speaking: Language shift in Austria. In David Sankoff (ed.), Linguistic variation: Models and methods, 227–238. New York: Academic Press.
Gal, Susan. 1979. Language shift: Social determinants of linguistic change in bilingual Austria. New York: Academic Press.
Gamandzori Joseph. 1992. L'articuation fleuve-rail au Congo. In Hélène d'Almeida-Topor, C. Chanso-Jabeur, and M. Lakroum (eds.), Les transports en Afrique (XIXe-Xxe siècle), 119–128. Paris: Harmattan.
Gerbault, Jeannine. 1987. Utilisation des langues et attitudes: la montée du sango. Bulletin de l'Observatoire du Français Contemporain en Afrique Noire.
Giles, Howard, Richard Bourhis, and Gloria Taylor. 1977. Toward a theory of language in ethnic group relations. In Howard Giles (ed.), Language, ethnicity and intergroup relations, 307–349. London and New York: Academic Press.
Giles, Howard, and B. Saint-Jacques, eds. 1979. Languages and ethnic relations. Oxford: Pergamon Press.
Greenberg, Joseph H. 1966. The languages of Africa. Bloomington: Indiana University Press.
Grolier Electronic Publishing, Inc. 1996. The 1996 Grolier multimedia encyclopedia.
Grosjean, François. 1982. Life with two languages: An introduction to bilingualism. Cambridge, Mass.: Harvard University Press.
Guilford, Joy P. 1956. Fundamental statistics in psychology and education. New York: McGraw-Hill, Inc.

Gumperz, John, and Dell Hymes, eds. 1972. Directions in sociolinguistics: The ethnography of communication. New York: Holt, Rinehart, and Winston.

Gumperz, John J., and R. Wilson. 1971. Convergence and creolization: A case from the Indo-Aryan/Dravidian border. In Dell Hymes (ed.), Pidginization and creolization of languages, 151–167. London: Cambridge University Press.

Harris, D. P. 1970. Report on an experimental group-administered memory span test. TESOL Quarterly 4:203–213.

Harrison, Andrew. 1983. A language testing handbook. London: Macmillan Press.

Haugen, Einar. 1981. Language fragmentation in Scandinavia: Revolt of the minorities. In Einar Haugen, J. Derrick McClure, and Derick S. Thomson (eds.), Minority languages today, 100–119. Edinburgh: Edinburgh University Press.

Holm, John A. 1988. Pidgins and Creoles I: Theory and structure. Cambridge: Cambridge University Press.

Holm, John A. 1989. Pidgins and Creoles II: Reference survey. Cambridge: Cambridge University Press.

Hornberger, Nancy. 1989. Continua of biliteracy. Review of Educational Research 59(3):271–296.

Hornberger, Nancy. 1990. Creating successful learning contexts for biliteracy. Penn Working Papers in Educational Linguistics 6(1):1–21.

Hornberger, Nancy, and Joel Hardman. 1994. Literacy as culteral practice and cognitive skill: Biliteracy in an ESL class and a GED program. In David Spener (ed.), Adult biliteracy in the United States. Center for Applied Linguistics and McHenry, Ill.: Delta Systems.

Humpstone, Henry Judson. 1917. Some aspects of the memory span test: A study in associability. Philadelphia: Psychological Clinic Press.

Hymes, Dell H. 1974. Foundations in sociolinguistics: An ethnographic approach. Philadelphia: University of Pennsylvania Press.

Jacobs, Joseph. 1887. Experiments on prehension. Mind 12:75–79.

Jacquot, André. 1961. Notes sur la situation du Sango à Bangui: résultats d'un sondage. Africa 31:158–166.

Jones, Bedwyr L. 1981. Welsh: Linguistic conservatism and shifting bilingualism. In E. Haugen, J. Derrick McClure, and Derick Thompson (eds.), Minority languages today. Edinburgh: Edinburgh University Press.

Kalck, Pierre. 1980. Historical dictionary of the Central African Republic (Translated by Thomas O'Toole). Metuchen, N.J. and London: The Scarecrow Press.

Koyt, Michel-Marie. 1994. Situation et politique linguistique de la République Centrafricaine. ms.
Kulik, Don. 1992. Language shift and cultural reproduction: Socialization, self, and syncretism in a Papua New Guinean village. Cambridge, U.K. and New York: Cambridge University Press.
Kuter, Lois. 1989. Breton vs. French: Language and the opposition of political, economic, social and cultural values. In Nancy C. Dorian (ed.), Investigating obsolescence: Studies in language contraction and death,75–89. Cambridge, U.K. and New York: Cambridge University Press.
Labov, William. 1965. On the mechanism of linguistic change. In Charles W. Kreidler (ed.), Georgetown University Monograph Series on Languages and Linguistics 18:91–114. (Reprinted in J. Gumperz and D. Hymes (eds.), Directions in sociolinguistics, 1972, 512–538.)
Labov, William. 1966. The social stratification of English in New York City. Washington: Center for Applied Linguistics.
Labov, William. 1972. Sociolinguistic patterns. Philadelphia: University of Pennsylvania Press.
Labov, William. 1981a. Resolving the Neogrammarian controversy. Language 57:267–308.
Labov, William. 1981b. What can be learned about change in progress from synchronic description? In David Sankoff and Henrietta Cedergren (eds.), Variation omnibus. Edmonton: Linguistic Research Inc.
Labov, William. 1995. Four riddles from the study of linguistic change in progress. ms.
Labov, William, Paul Cohen, Clarence Robins, and John Lewis. 1968. A study of the non-standard English of Negro and Puerto Rican speakers in New York City I: Phonological and gramatical analysis. Philadelphia, Penn.: The U.S. Regional Survey.
Lado, Robert. 1965. Memory span as a factor in second language learning. International Review of Applied Linguistics 3:123–129.
Liberson, Stanley. 1965. Bilingualism in Montreal: A demographic analysis. American Journal of Sociology 71:10–25.
Liberson, S. 1982. Forces affecting language spread: Some basic propositions. In Robert L. Cooper (ed.), Language spread: Studies in diffusion and social change. Bloomington: Indiana University Press.
Lieberson, Stanley, and Lynn Hansen. 1974. National development, mother tongue diversity, and the comparative study of nations. American Sociological Review 39:523–41.
Mackey, William F., and Donald G. Cartwright. 1979. Geocoding language loss from census data. In William R. Mackey and Jacob Ornstein (eds.),

Sociolinguistic studies in language contact: Methods and cases, 69–96. The Hague: Mouton.

Miller, George, and S. Isard. 1963. Some perceptual consequences of linguistic rules. Journal of Verbal Learning and Verbal Behavior 2:217–228.

Monino, Yves, ed. 1988. Lexique comparatif des langues Oubanguennes. Paris: L.A.P.A.C.

Moser, Rosmarie. 1992. Sociolinguistic dynamics of Sango. M.A. thesis. La Trobe University: Bundoora, Victoria, Australia.

Natalicio, Diana S. 1977. Sentence repetition as a language assessment technique: Some issues and applications. The Bilingual Review 4:107–112.

Nelson, Quentin D. 1952. Linguistic problems in Ngbandi. The Bible Translator 3:31–45.

Pandharipande, Rajeshwari. 1992. Language shift in India: Issues and implications. In Willem Fase, Koen Jaspaert, and Sjaak Kroon (eds.), Maintenance and loss of minority languages, 253–275. Amsterdam and Philadelphia: John Benjamins.

Paul, Hermann. 1880. Prinzipien der sprachgeschichte. Tübingen: Max Niemeyer Verlag. Sixth Edition (unchanged), 1960.

Paulston, Christina Bratt. 1992. Linguistic minorities and language policies: Four case studies. In Willem Fase, Koen Jaspaert, and Sjaak Kroon (eds.), Maintenance and loss of minority languages, 55–79. Amsterdam and Philadelphia: John Benjamins.

Pool, Jonathan, 1972. National development and language diversity, In Joshua Fishman (ed.), Advances in the sociology of language 2, 213–230. The Hague: Mouton.

Radloff, Carla F. 1991. Sentence repetition testing for studies of community bilingualism. The Summer Institute of Linguistics and The University of Texas at Arlington Publications in Linguistics 104. Dallas.

Recensement générale de la population. 1988. Sécretaire d'Etat au Plan aux Statistiques et à la Coopération Internationale, Bureau Central de Recensement. Central African Republic.

Roberts. 1993. Ph.D. dissertation. University of Pennsylvania.

Romain, Suzanne. 1989. Pidgins, creoles, immigrant, and dying languages. In Nancy C. Dorian (ed.), Investigating obsolescence: Studies in language contraction and death, 369–383. Cambridge and New York: Cambridge University Press.

Romaine, Suzanne. 1995. Bilingualism (second edition). Oxford, U.K. and Cambridge, Mass.: Blackwell.

Rubin, Joan. 1961. Bilingualism in Paraguay. Anthropological Linguistics 4:52–58.

Rubin, Joan. 1968. Bilingual usage in Paraguay. In Joshua Fishman, (ed.), Readings in the sociology of language, 512–530. The Hague: Mouton.
Samarin, William J. 1955. Sango, an African lingua franca. Word 11(2):254–367.
Samarin, William J. 1970. Sango: Langue de l'Afrique Centrale. Leiden: E. J. Brill.
Samarin, William J. 1982. Colonization and pidginization on the Ubangi River. Journal of African Languages and Linguistics 4:1–42.
Samarin, William J. 1986. French and Sango in the Central African Republic. Anthropological Linguistics 28(3):377–387.
Sankoff, David, and Suzanne Laberge. 1978. The linguistic market and the statistical explanation of variability. In David Sankoff (ed.), Linguistic variation: Models and methods, 239–250. New York: Academic Press.
Sankoff, Gillian. 1977. Creolization and syntactic change in New Guina Tok Pisin. In Ben G. Blount and Mary Sanches (eds.), Sociocultural dimensions of language change, 119–129. New York: Academic Press.
Schach, Paul, ed. 1980. Languages in conflict: Linguistic acculturation on the Great Plains. Lincoln: University of Nebraska Press.
Scheibner-Herzig, Gudrun, Heike Sauerbrey, and Siegfried Kokoschka. 1991. Repetition: A means to predict foreign language oral proficiency. International Review of Applied Linguistics 29:227–240.
Spener, David, ed. 1994. Adult Biliteracy in the United States. Center for Applied Linguistics and McHenry, Ill.: Delta Systems.
Sridhar, S. N. 1987. Language variation, attitudes, and rivalry: The spread of Hindi in India. In Peter H. Lowenberg (ed.), Language spread and language policy: Issues implications, and case studies, 300–319. Washington D.C.: Georgetown University Press.
Stevenson, Douglas K. 1981. Beyond faith and face validity: The multitrait-multimethod matrix and the convergent and discriminant validity of oral proficiency tests. In Adrian Palmer, Peter Groot, and George Trosper (eds.), The construct validation of tests of communicative competence. Washington, D.C.: Teachers of English to Speakers of Other Languages.
Taber, Charles R. 1964. French loan words in Sango: A statistical analysis of incidence. Hartford, Connecticut: Hartford Seminary Foundation.
Taber, Charles R. 1979. French loan words in Sango: The motivation of lexical borrowing. In Ian F. Hancock (ed.), Readings in Creole studies, 189–197. Ghent: Scientific Publishers.

Thomason, Sarah G., and Terrence Kaufman. 1988. Language contact, creolization, and genetic linguistics. Berkeley: University of California Press.

Trudgil, Peter. 1974. Linguistic change and diffusion: Description and explanation in sociolinguistic dialect geography. Language in Society 3:215–246.

Trudgill, Peter, and Giannes A. Tzavaras. 1977. Why Albanian-Greeks are not Albanians: Language shift in Attica and Biotia. In Howard Giles (ed.), Language, ethnicity and intergroup relations, 171–185. London: Academic Press.

Wardhaugh, Ronald. 1987. Languages in competition: Dominance, diversity, and decline. Oxford and New York: Basil Blackwell.

Watson, Seosamh. 1989. Scottish and Irish Gaelic: The giant's bed-fellows. In Nancy C. Dorian (ed.), Investigating obsolescence: Studies in language contraction and death, 41–59. Cambridge and New York: Cambridge University Press.

Weinreich, Uriel. 1953. Languages in contact. New York: Linguistic Circle of New York.

Weinreich, Uriel, William Labov, and Marvin Herzog. 1968. Empirical foundations of a theory of language change. In Winfred P. Lehmann and Yakov Malkiel (eds.), Directions for historical linguistics: A symposium, 95–195. Austin: University of Texas Press.

Wenezoui, Martine. 1989. Les langues parlées. Littérature Centrafricaine 97. Avril-Mai. 19–22.

Wetherill, Barrie. 1992. Report on an analysis of data from the bilingualism test in Cameroon, 1991 (BITECOSTUG). ms.

Williams, Frederick. 1968. Reasoning with statistics: Simplified examples in communications research. New York: Holt, Rinehart, and Winston.

Williamson, Robert C. 1991. Minority languages and bilingualism: Case studies in maintenance and shift. Norwood, N.J.: Ablex Publishing Corporation.

Index

A

AAVE 33
age 13, 15, 29, 32, 56, 58–59, 61–67, 74–75, 87, 95–96, 99, 104–105, 119, 122, 139
ANOVA 59, 61–65, 67–68, 70–72

B

Bangui 5, 7, 11–13, 16, 19, 38, 58–59, 63–64, 66, 68–74, 78, 80–81, 83, 85, 87, 92, 95, 109–110
Baratz 34
bilingual 7, 13, 21, 28–29, 81, 114–115
biliteracy 114–115
Boltanski 22
Bossangoa 39, 55
Bossangua 87, 93
Bouquiaux 6
Bourdieu 22–23, 30
Bruel 5, 8
Buraka 8–9

C

children 7, 11, 13, 17, 26, 34, 85–87, 98, 115, 121–122
choices 1, 22–24, 26, 29–31, 66, 97–99, 101, 118–121
Christian 3, 10–11, 37–38
cluster analysis 78–80, 82
code-switching 9, 18, 30
Coulmas 104–105

D

Dacko 6
development 2–4, 7, 9, 37, 39, 42, 47–48, 50, 52, 54, 56, 58, 83–84, 89, 103–111, 113–116
difficulty level 42–43, 45, 49, 52, 54
diglossic 98
Diki-Kidiri 6
discrimination 50
discrimination index 43–45, 47, 49–53
domains 1, 13, 16, 1–20, 29, 95

Dorian 100

E

ecology of language 22
education 6–7, 9, 16, 23, 25, 57, 59, 61–62, 64, 68, 70–75, 85–86, 95–96, 107, 111
Educational Testing Services 41
Edwards 24, 30, 104

F

Fasold 23–25, 30, 35
Fishman 19, 25, 29
French 5–10, 12, 14–16, 18–19, 23, 37, 39, 73–74, 83–88, 95, 107, 113, 115

G

Gal 21–22, 25, 27– 29
Gapun 26
Gbanziri 6, 8–9
Gbaya 77, 79, 87
Gbeya 10
gender 13, 59, 63–65, 84
Gender 63–64
geographic distance 59, 80–81
Gerbault 16
German 21, 28
Giles, Bourhis, and Taylor 20
government 7, 10, 12, 19, 23, 58, 67–68, 83, 86, 88–89, 106–110, 112
Greenberg 8, 76
Grosjean 24
group behavior 96, 101, 118
Guarani 20–21
Gumperz 25, 29

H

Harris 35
Haugen 22
Herzog 27, 117, 119
Holm 6
Hungarian 21, 28

I

ILA 7

J

Jacquot 12–14, 18

K

Kalck 6
Kare 11, 77
Kaufman 25
Koyt 7–8, 18–19
Kulick 25–26

L

Laberge 23
Labov 15, 25, 27, 29, 117, 119–120
Labov, Cohen, Robins, and Lewis 33, 34
Lado 34–35
language change 2–4, 23, 27, 29–30, 32, 74, 96, 97, 103, 116–119, 121, 123
language loss 19, 24–25
language loyalty 100, 113–115
language preservation 104, 108
Liberson 23, 25
Lieberson and Hansen 105
linguistic market 23, 30, 67
linguistic relatedness 59, 76–80
Londo 55

M

Manja 13
memory span 34–35
mimicry 35, 99, 116, 120–121
Monino 76
Moser 16–18
motivations 2, 12, 14–15, 25–27, 29, 31–32, 96–101, 103–104, 106, 108–120, 122

N

Natalicio 35
national identity 86–87
national language 6–8, 86–87, 108
national unity 12, 111
Ngbandi 6, 9, 77–78

O

occupation 5–6, 8–9, 57–59, 61–62, 67–68, 96
official language 5–6, 8, 18, 107
origins of Sango 6, 8
orthography 8

P

Pandharipande 25
parents language 58
Paul 116–118
Paulston 98
predictability index 47, 51–54, 56
prestige 2, 8, 10–11, 14–15, 22, 28–29, 68, 88, 97–99
proficiency levels 41

R

Radloff 3, 33, 35–39, 42–47, 50–51
recorded 37–38, 40, 57
regression 46, 48, 59, 61–65, 67–73, 76, 78, 81, 96, 105
residence 57–59, 61–62, 68–72, 74
residence history 57–59, 61–62, 69–70, 75, 95
resistance 113–115
Roberts 121
RPE 38–42, 46–57, 73–74
Rubin 20, 29

S

Samarin 5–6, 8–16
Sango 2–3, 5–19, 31, 33, 37–40, 43, 45–48, 50, 52, 55–56, 59, 61, 64–75, 77–90, 92–93, 95, 98–99, 107–110, 113–115
Sankoff 23, 25
Scheibner-Herzig, Sauerbrey, and Kokoschka 35
schools 12, 74, 84–86, 107, 115
shift 2–4, 11, 19–32, 69, 74–75, 80, 85, 88, 95–98, 100–101, 103–104, 108, 110, 113–116, 119, 121–123
Spanish 20–21
spouse's language 62

spread 1–5, 8–9, 11–13, 15, 1–25, 29, 31, 33, 66–67, 69, 76, 79, 81–82, 88, 92–93, 95–97, 101, 103, 10–111, 114–115, 121–122
SRT 2–3, 33, 35–37, 39–40, 42–59, 61–76, 78–79, 82, 85, 95–96, 100

T
Taber 14
Thomason 25
Tok Pisin 26
Trudgill 81
two-value scoring system 47–50, 53

V
values 2, 17, 25–26, 41, 62–63, 88, 103, 106, 108, 113, 119, 121–123
variables 2, 23, 31, 59, 62,–64, 66, 78, 118–119, 121–123

W
Wardhaugh 24
Weinreich 10, 14–15, 100, 117
Wenezoui 18
Wetherill 47, 50

Y
Yalouké 55

SIL International
Publications in Sociolinguistics
Recent Publications

7. **The dynamics of Sango language spread** by Mark E. Karan, 2001.
6. **K'iche': A study in the sociology of language** by M. Paul Lewis, 2001.
5. **The same but different: Language use and attitudes in four communities of Burkina Faso** by Stuart Showalter, 2001.
4. **Ashéninka stories of change** by Ronald James Anderson, 2001.
3. **Assessing ethnolinguistic vitality: Theory and practice** Gloria Kindell and M. Paul Lewis, eds., 2000.
2. **The early days of sociolinguistics** Christina Bratt Paulston and G. Richard Tucker, eds., 1997
1. **North Sulawesi language survey** by Scott Merrifield and Martinus Sales, 1996.

For further information or a full listing of SIL publications contact:

International Academic Bookstore
Summer Institute of Linguistics
7500 W. Camp Wisdom Road
Dallas, TX 75236-5699

Voice: 972-708-7404
Fax: 972-708-7363
Email: academic_books@sil.org
Internet: http://www.sil.org

www.ingramcontent.com/pod-product-compliance
Lightning Source LLC
Chambersburg PA
CBHW070334230426
43663CB00011B/2304